IMAGES OF
WESTMORLAND

Sutton Publishing Limited
Phoenix Mill · Thrupp · Stroud
Gloucestershire · GL5 2BU

First published 2002

Half-title page: The coat of arms of Westmorland County Council (1889–1974). The County Council was formed under the Local Government Act of 1888 and was granted the Coat of Arms by the College of Heralds in 1926. It ceased to be used officially in 1974 when the administrative county of Westmorland became part of the new local government county of Cumbria.
Title page: St Patrick's Well at Patterdale comes to us in modern times as a symbol of the early Christian influence in the then wild moorland area we now call the Lake District. This private photograph from 1 June 1903 shows visitors to Patterdale posing against the nineteenth-century canopy over the ancient well.

British Library Cataloguing in Publication Data
A catalogue record for this book is available from the British Library.

ISBN 0-7509-2995-2

Typeset in 10.5/13.5 Photina.
Typesetting and origination by
Sutton Publishing Limited.
Printed and bound in England by
J.H. Haynes & Co. Ltd, Sparkford.

This book is dedicated to my wife Jean, who always dreamed of living in Westmorland and achieved her objective in our marriage.

Lowther Castle, near Penrith, was the seat of the Earls of Lonsdale who were the local government of most of Westmorland for many hundreds of years. Lowther Castle was stripped of its roof and fittings after the 'sale of the century' of the contents in April, May and June 1947 and now stands as a ruin. The family and Lonsdale Estates continue to have a presence in the modern county of Cumbria.

IN OLD PHOTOGRAPHS

IMAGES OF WESTMORLAND

JOHN MARSH

SUTTON PUBLISHING

The Mallerstang postman, 'Awd Cooper' from Kirkby Stephen, walked the valley to Thrang and back six days a week, extending his trip on three days to include Aisgill moor. He was an ex-Militia man from the time of the Boer War who had strong views on many subjects, which he freely offered to the valley residents as he delivered their post. Truly a Westmorland character from the first decades of the twentieth century. (*Anon/J. Marsh Collection*)

CONTENTS

Lord Lonsdale, Hugh Cecil Lowther, the 'Yellow Earl' is seen examining the card at Grasmere Sports in the early twentieth century. The 5th Lord Lonsdale was very much a sportsman, and he and his wife were to be seen at many Westmorland events up to the time of the the Second World War. (*Mallinson of Windermere/J. Marsh Collection*)

INTRODUCTION

At the beginning of the 1990s I was asked by Sutton Publishing to produce three books that covered the lost county of Westmorland. These appeared as *South Westmorland Villages* in 1991, and *The Westmorland Lakes* and *Eden Valley, Westmorland* in 1992. These three books have been out of print for some time and are difficult to obtain. Interest in Westmorland has continued to grow into the twenty-first century and requests for a book on the whole lost county have been many. Compiling these books is a task that I enjoy and thus we now have *Images of Westmorland*. It covers the whole of the county but, obviously, not in as much depth as the previous three books.

In 1974 the fell-walking author and writer, Alfred Wainwright, expressed much dismay that the Local Government Commission was to 'wipe Westmorland off the map' and along with it the boroughs of Kendal and Appleby, which had existed some centuries before the inception of the county of Westmorland. He decided to write a book, *Westmorland Heritage*, and this appeared in 1975. The limited edition soon sold out and copies now fetch large prices when they can be found for sale. The demise of Westmorland changed the type of book that was coming from the pen of this shy genius. The map of Westmorland, 'suitable for framing', was also a success and then *Three Westmorland Rivers* in 1979 continued the lost county theme. *Kendal in the Nineteenth Century* in 1977 satisfied the urge to record the lost Royal Borough of Kendal, which, for many years, Wainwright had served as Treasurer. For some reason that will now never be known 'AW' drew me into the production of his 'heritage' books. This proved to be an experience I will never forget, as I watched project after project come to full production on the presses of the *Westmorland Gazette*. A whole department there survived on AW's output. It was AW who suggested to me that as Percy Duff, his professional assistant and later his successor, was busy with his wife collecting old photographs of Kendal, that I might collect pictures of the villages of Westmorland. This I did, and as a result had many years of great interest and happiness as I assembled the photographs that have appeared in many of the Sutton old photograph books. This opened the door to many friendships and contacts that I would never otherwise have had.

Westmorland was a name dating back to the period just after the Roman occupation of Britain, when the north of modern England was part of the Scottish kingdom of Strathclyde and the kingdom of Cumbria was part of Scottish lands. There are many fables and folk yarns about the early history of Westmorland, but the name first appears in written documents as 'Westmoringaland' in 966. There is much yet to be discovered regarding the true story of Westmorland, but the Barony of Appleby and the Barony of Kendal continued the story through the middle ages into the eighteenth century when other power bases started to exist that transformed the county into a modern entity.

Landowners such as the Lowthers, the Broughams, the Hothfields, the Stricklands, the Cliffords and the Howards slowly gave way politically to new groups such as the Whigs and the Quakers who transformed county ways, although patronage from the old lords was still much sought after. This odd system of underfunding together with patronage continued well into modern times, so much so that the Royal Commission that was looking into boundary changes in the mid-1960s remarked: 'Taken as a whole it is unlike any other county in England; it has neither the problems nor the resources that come from large scale urbanisation; owing to its geography, boundary changes would only have a limited effect on the services at the point where they are received. On the other hand, many people who give their services might be discouraged from doing so if their county were divided or attached to another one.' In spite of this warning about the loss of patronage Westmorland became part of Cumbria in 1974, but its inhabitants continued, as of old, to seek patronage from their old leaders without realising that political times had changed and that their patrons were probably as hard up as the cause for which they were seeking assistance.

Westmorland continues as a quite distinct area. The Royal Commission remarked: 'It would form a division of any major unit to which it might be transferred', and while this was never achieved in the set-up of Cumbria County Council it has managed to be deprived of as much funding by the new council as it ever was by the government in the days of Westmorland County Council. It was always cheap to run. This area reminds the visitor of childhood visits to a widowed aunt who tries to hide her poverty by pride. The richness of the stories from the old lady make up for lack of services which she might once have wished to provide.

Like many stories from an old lady, Westmorland's written history has to be taken with a large pinch of salt. Much has been written to fit into the politics of the age. The Normans obliterated the Anglo-Saxon and earlier histories, while Reformation politics replaced the medieval Roman Catholic times as though they had never been, and as modern times came near the process went on. In the nineteenth century, much of the history was put together by romantics and wasn't based on factual documentation. Today a history book of repute is eagerly awaited by the residents of the lands once called Westmorland, but instead a number of articles and books appear that have to be found to obtain part of the story – but there is much yet to be discovered, in particular the early history which probably only archaeologists will be able to unearth. This compilation of early photographs is not the long-awaited history of Westmorland that only academics can provide but is a collection of images from the past – some valuable primary sources, with historical material as well as a rich vein of pure nostalgia.

So, from the land of the Lowthers, their employee William Wordsworth and their neighbour – 'the man who broke the bank at Monte Carlo' – Lord Brougham, as well as the Peter Rabbit fables and their author Mrs Heelis (Beatrix Potter), and from the adopted county of Alfred Wainwright, fell-walking writer and genius, I offer *Images of Westmorland*, now a lost county but one that has survived as a place to love. I hope my pictures show the reader why.

John Marsh
Spring 2002

1

Transport

The Lancaster to Kendal Canal, opened fully in 1819, is seen here at Stainton south of Kendal in the late nineteenth century. The barge, called the *Herbert*, belonged to S. Kent, and was on contract to the London & North Western Railway which then owned the canal. Workmen are clearing the canal of vegetation. Its closure took place at the end of the Second World War when transport of coal to Kendal Gas Works was transferred to road. The canal was very much a feature of south Westmorland for over a hundred years and plans are now in place to reopen it as a tourist attraction before 2010. (*Anon/J. Marsh Collection*)

Toll bars, gates or booths were a common sight on Westmorland roads when the turnpike system was in operation. People wanting to use a road paid a fee at the toll house, but many locals found a way round the gates and the system just did not function in the way intended. The Westmorland Quarter Sessions took over the road system for a short time in the nineteenth century but in 1889 responsibility passed to the new Westmorland County Council. Above we see the toll booth on what later became the A6 road at Levens Hall. Below is the toll booth on the original Heron Skye to Eamont Bridge turnpike road, at the south end of the Burton in Kendal village of Heronsyke. Many toll booth houses still survive as private dwellings throughout the old county, but both those shown here were destroyed in the early twentieth century. (*Above and below: J. Marsh Collection*)

Stepping stones date back to antiquity and usually mark the site of a ford, which nowadays will have been replaced by a bridge. The two sets of stepping stones shown here have different stories to tell us. Above is the set of stones at the River Lowther crossing near Shap Abbey where the ancient road from Kendal to Penrith passed the abbey in medieval times. They were very much a tourist attraction in the nineteenth century when visitors to Shap Abbey ruins included them in their visit. This must have proved a nuisance when some of the stones were removed, making a dry foot crossing impossible. Below can be seen the set of stones where the River Rothay is crossed on the ancient route from Ambleside to Coniston. These stones have been part of tourist trips to Ambleside from well before the days of William Wordsworth, offering the intrepid the chance to test their nerve. Any attempt to remove them today would cause an outcry. (*Above: Anon/J. Marsh Collection. Below: Brunskill of Windermere/J. Marsh Collection*)

Below: Rydal Moss near Grasmere had a very different appearance in the mid-nineteenth century when photographer Payne-Jennings visited on a tour. This resulted in his publication of a mid-Victorian album of superb photographs of the Lake District. The scene at White Moss includes his two photographer's vans which were part of the equipment of early photographers as the large glass plate images required rapid processing. The amazing results of this processing can be seen in many modern picture collections and a number are to be found in this book. The quality of prints from nearly 150 years ago brings that period of Westmorland history alive. (*Payne-Jennings/From the collection of the late Olive Wilson*)

Opposite: Rydal, at the foot of the lane to Rydal Hall, and Rydal Mount and church, where a nineteenth-century party stop on a trip round the lakes by horse coach. Horse-drawn charabancs like these were a common sight on the unmade Westmorland roads for over a hundred years. If it rained everybody got wet. (*Anon/J. Marsh Collection*)

The Prince of Wales Hotel at Grasmere now carries a different name but can still be recognised from the days of another mid-Victorian photographer who did not leave his name with his picture. The hotel 'bus' (with seating on top) draws towards the coach entrance of the hotel, which was below the large sign reading 'Brown's Prince of Wales Lake Hotel'. Browns also had an hotel in Ambleside and became very much involved in tourist coaching. The business name lives on even today in modern motor coaches. Hotel bus travel was part of a package holiday provided, no doubt, by the railway company, and also catered for 'free' travellers visiting the Lake District and arriving at Windermere railway station, where the driver would seek their custom for his hotel. (*Anon/J. Marsh Collection*)

Pony and trap was the common way of travel for many until the arrival of the motor car, and above we see Mary Wakefield of Sedgwick House in the south of the county in her trap near Natland. This village is on the ancient road into Kendal which had become a lane. The replacement turnpike road from Burton in Kendal through Endmoor was in due course replaced by the modern A6, and later the M6. Mary Wakefield became famous for the introduction of choral music competitions in the area, which tradition spread all over England. Below, the farming family at Natland Mill Beck Farm pose in their farmyard with their neat trap. This would also double as a milk float with a churn on the back for daily milk deliveries in the district. Holly Chapman, née Webster, poses at the reins. (*Above and below: Anon/J. Marsh Collection*)

Carts came in various designs, being built to individual order by the local joiner, wheelwright and blacksmith. Above is a farm cart with extended sides, which would carry almost anything for the farmer and was widely used to spread manure in the fields. It is seen on the road into Hartsop, Patterdale. Below, an itinerant fruit and vegetable trader, W. Rigg of Grasmere, is seen on the road in Langdale, *c.* 1905. His cart with its wider axle was obviously designed to give a stable ride for his wares on the unmade roads. (*Above: Lowe of Patterdale/J. Marsh Collection. Below: Anon/collection of the late J. Story*)

Horse and carriage trips were organised by hotels and travel companies to cater for all requirements. Above we see a group on a small coach at the Dungeon Ghyll Hotel in Langdale in about 1900, and below two charabanc carriages wait at the Kirkstone Pass Inn while their horses are fed and watered after the steep climb to the summit, *c.* 1910. There were many accidents, which were reported in the local papers. (*Above: Atkinson of Ulverston/J. Marsh Collection. Below: Anon/J. Marsh Collection*)

Horses in the Lake District part of Westmorland could expect to be used on a wide range of tasks, which, with the hills, were all hard work. Above can be seen a team of horses near Grasmere drawing trees to the sawmill. The same horses would have been used before the journey to lift the logs on to the wagon. Below, tourist coaches are seen gathered outside the offices of Brown's coaches in The Square at Ambleside. On the other side of the road were the offices of Rigg's, who ran not only holiday coaches and hotels but also the Royal Mail coaches from Windermere station to Keswick. Their drivers wore a distinctive uniform of red jacket and grey/white top hat. One of them can be seen striding across the road. Visitors to Ambleside hotels were offered a number of tours (called rounds) on awful roads to many different locations. (*Above and below: Anon/J. Marsh Collection*)

A car being helped from a snowdrift on top of Dunmail Raise in 1937 shows how the Westmorland horses were needed even into the days of the motor car. No details surrounding the incident come with the picture, but no doubt the modern man at the wheel of the car would be grateful for the old technology coming to his aid. (*Anon/J. Marsh Collection*)

Opposite: Heversham is the site of a pre-Norman Christian settlement and its holy well of St Mary can be seen on the right of the road, in its days as a horse trough on the main road through the village, which became the A6. The old Blue Bell Inn can be seen on the left, where the weary traveller could also enjoy a drink. The holy well horse trough can still be seen but the Blue Bell has been closed: a new inn of the same name was opened on the side of Heversham bypass road, which was built in the 1930s. Kendal architect John F. Curwen found the road at Heversham intolerable, and created a fuss to have the A6 moved out of the village. (*Crosland of Arnside/J. Marsh Collection*)

Cows paddle in the river Belah at Beetham in the south of the county on the site of the Beetham ford, in May 1920. The Beetham bridge nearby on the A6 gained a notoriety through the 1930s to 1950s for terrible accidents where many people died. Lorries driven too long by tired drivers came to grief on the parapets of the bridge, and many did not survive to explain what happened. This ford has a history from the Dark Ages when a large battle is reputed to have taken place there. As a policeman remarked in the 1960s, 'The Westmorland County Highways Department continues the slaughter.' It was not until the M6 motorway was built in the 1970s that the carnage at Beetham ceased. (*Simcoe of Kendal/ J. Marsh Collection*)

Temple Sowerby has a history dating back to the days of the Knights Templar in the early medieval period. Unfortunately it was also on an ancient east–west road, which became a Roman road and much later a turnpike road. Not much improved, this road continued into the twentieth century unmade, as can be seen in this photograph from the early years of that century. The turnpike road in due course became the modern A66, now much used by gigantic lorries. The village has been ruined and polluted since the inception of the internal combustion engine, and even as this book is being written (except for the tarmac roadway and today's horrendous traffic) the view remains little different, an indictment of the poverty of Westmorland County Council highways policies. (*Anon/J. Marsh Collection*)

The Plough Inn at Selside on the A6 took its name from an inn on the pre-turnpike road that can still be traced in fields just behind. On its way over the Shap Fells the A6 passed a number of wayside inns, of which the Plough was one of the favourites. The opening of the M6 in the 1970s changed everything, and the Plough never really recovered its lost business. It is now being redeveloped as housing. (*Simcoe of Kendal/J. Marsh Collection*)

The Lancaster to Kendal canal near Holme, *c.* 1900. This photograph shows the waterway, the towpath and the north–south telegraph system that used the canal route. This section of canal caused many problems, as the bank let water leak into the properties on the west side. A waterpipe was installed when canal traffic ceased in the late 1940s. (*Anon/J. Marsh Collection*)

The Hincaster tunnel on the Lancaster to Kendal canal, *c.* 1900, when the canal was still a working waterway. On the right can be seen the outline of the horse path over the hill, marked by the row of trees and bushes. The horse was taken off the tow rope before the barge entered the tunnel, and the barge was 'walked through' or pulled through the tunnel by ropes fixed to the tunnel walls. Even though the canal no longer exists this piece of eighteenth-century engineering has been listed by the government, and discussions are currently in hand about its inclusion in the canal that will reopen a waterway to Kendal from the south in about 2005. (*Anon/J. Marsh Collection*)

Kirkby Stephen annual fair on Hills Bottom field was approached by vehicles using a ford across the River Eden. Above can be seen Jeffries' heavy lorry towing their living van over the ford in 1954. The lorry was probably ex-War Department, as many showmen had swapped their pre-war steam engines for the big diesel lorries available at war's end in 1945, when many fighting vehicles were being sold by the government. Below can be seen the same ford in earlier years when one of the giant showman's steam engines tows its load to the showfield. In this picture it is Taylor Brothers' Galloping Horses on the trailer. The steam engine would provide power for the roundabouts as well as lighting for the showmen's stalls. (*Above: J. Marsh/J. Marsh Collection. Below: Anon/G. Dawson Collection*)

Windermere Ferry is shown here as it existed from medieval times until the nineteenth century, when steam power was introduced. Above, the rowing boat ferry is seen loaded with a carriage and a horse and cart, and below the ferry is being loaded. It is said that any passengers would, like it or not, be asked to assist with the oars. In 1870 the rowing boat ferry was finally replaced with a ferry powered by a steam engine. (*Above and below: Anon/J. Marsh Collection*)

The Swan was a Furness Railway steamer that carried passengers from Lakeside to Ambleside, stopping at a number of piers on the way. The unscheduled stop pictured here was on 26 September 1909. The boat had left Ambleside at 7.15 pm and called at the Low Wood Pier, but 200 yards beyond Low Wood she ran into a thick bank of fog and as a result soon ran aground at Belle Grange on the opposite side of the lake. There were seven passengers on board with the crew and Captain Eccles. A member of the crew got ashore and borrowed a ladder from Belle Grange, allowing the passengers and the rest of the crew to get ashore. They walked 2 miles in pouring rain to the Ferry Hotel where they were refreshed and rowed over to Bowness (still in heavy rain). This photograph was taken the following day. The Swan was refloated on 29 September to resume her duties, which lasted until she was scrapped in 1938 – having lasted since 1869. (*Herbert of Windermere/J. Marsh Collection*)

The *Tern* sailed Windermere lake for many years with the *Swan* as part of the Furness Railway fleet. She was popular as she was a twin screw 'puffer' until her engine was replaced after the Second World War by British Railways when a diesel engine was installed. Built in 1891 she still serves the lake with a very different appearance now to how she was originally constructed. Here she is seen at Ambleside pier in the early decades of the twentieth century with a typical overload of passengers. (*Anon/J. Marsh Collection*)

The barbed humour of Cynicus postcards was usually directed at transport of the early twentieth century. Branch railway lines were a typical target, but overloaded steamers on Lake Windermere were also lampooned. Here we see 'The last boat Ambleside to Bowness', which no doubt made the point but would also sell very well in the 'wish you were here' market at both Ambleside and Bowness as well as on the steamers. Note that the boat is a paddle steamer, as were the lake steam boats in the nineteenth century (see p. 50). (*Cynicus/J. Marsh Collection*)

Ullswater was on the border between the adjoining counties of Cumberland and Westmorland, and yet Westmorland appears on both shores, as the boundary was a mid-lake affair. This was unlike Windermere where the whole of the lake was in Westmorland and much of the shore was in Lancashire. Here we see two Westmorland scenes, with the Ullswater steamer *Raven* which was built in 1889, leaving the Ullswater Hotel pier at Patterdale in 1909 (above) and (left) entering Howtown bay on the opposite shore a few years later. Both locations were in Westmorland. The problems of jurisdiction over this eccentric boundary were many but, in general, were sorted out by a high degree of cooperation between the two counties. (*Above: Lowe of Patterdale/J. Marsh Collection. Left: Reeds of Penrith/J. Marsh Collection*)

Above, inset: Windermere was used for many speed record attempts, but the attempt by Sir Henry Segrave on Friday 13 June 1930 was notable in a way that no one involved would have wished. The speedboat *Miss England II* flipped over at speed and Sir Henry and his mechanic Vic Halwell were killed, and another member of the crew, Michael Willcocks, was injured but survived. The scene shows the upturned boat with rescue craft at the scene of the disaster. (*Anon/J. Marsh Collection*)

Levens bridge in the south of the county was originally a narrow affair designed for horses and carriages, so when motorised transport appeared on the A6 the passage of the local K bus reduced the traffic to one way. The destination of the bus was to be seen on the small notice in the front window – it was probably bound for Milnthorpe from Kendal. The K indicated the Kendal Motor Bus company, which ran services in the area from the 1920s until taken over by the Ribble Bus Company of Preston. (*Anon/J. Marsh Collection*)

The Windermere based Magnet Bus Company run by Mr C. Head also took parties on away-day trips. This one was to Southport, although the sign in the window indicates the usual work for the vehicle. Mr Head had joined in the lucrative trade from Windermere railway station to Bowness promenade to take thousands of holiday visitors who arrived by the trainload at Windermere station only to find that it was a couple of miles to the lake. This business had been carried on by Rigg's and others for many years using horse charabancs. (*Rigby of Southport/J. Marsh Collection*)

German superiority in motor charabanc manufacture is indicated in these two photographs taken on Kirkstone pass, showing Daimler charabanc coaches. Above, the Ulverston Cooperative staff outing over Kirkstone pass is seen at the summit, and below another coach with a Lancashire registration (TB 1413) pulls up towards the summit with Brotherswater in the background. Note that on the unmade Westmorland road both charabancs have hard tyres and, no doubt, the passengers would have had a hard ride. Both pictures are from just after the First World War. (*Above: Anon/J. Marsh Collection. Below: Mayson of Keswick/J. Marsh Collection*)

Yachting on Windermere, *c.* 1900. Alfred Pettitt of Keswick's photograph shows a Windermere class racing yacht in full flight under full sail. Its speed would easily exceed 10 miles per hour. These yachts required a high degree of skill to sail, or even keep afloat, as a well-recognised characteristic of the class was that, in trouble, the boat sank like a stone, owing no doubt to the heavy keel required to balance the sails. The photographer Alfred Pettitt was originally from Grasmere where he learned his skills with the local schoolmaster William Baldry. This was without doubt the cradle of early Lakeland photography in the mid-nineteenth century. Pettitt opened an art gallery in Grasmere in 1853, and when Baldry took up photography and later opened a stationer's shop in 1856 he worked on the new art with him. In 1858 he moved to St John's Street, Keswick, where he could sell both his paintings and his photographs in his shop. He has been called the 'father of Lakeland photography', which title should possibly belong to William Baldry, but he was without doubt the first photographer in Keswick. His photographs always have an 'arty' finish to them, as this yacht picture demonstrates. (*A. Pettitt/ J. Marsh Collection*)

Crag Brow, Bowness-on-Windermere, with a Ribble Bus Company Leyland service bus en route to Ulverston, probably from Ambleside. These between the war buses were in general service throughout Westmorland wherever Ribble ran, and provided a degree of comfort never before experienced on Westmorland roads. (*Leyland Bus Company/J. Marsh Collection*)

The Magnet bus from Windermere station to the promenade at Bowness was a winner for Mr C. Head, who is seen here with a later vehicle than that seen on page 28. By this time both he and his vehicle were licensed under Public Service Vehicle regulations which had to be complied with if a service was run. Note the proprietor's name and address at the bottom of the entrance steps. Times were a-changing, as was the road surface seen here. (*Anon/ J. Marsh Collection*)

The Heversham bypass under construction in 1927. When Kendal architect John Flavel Curwen left Kendal to live in Heversham he was disgusted at pollution from the A6, which ran along the main street of the village – and in particular outside the Heversham church (see p. 19). He lobbied the County Council to change the situation and thus the new road was planned and constructed – a remarkable achievement in Westmorland. It is a pity that while resident in Kendal he had not carried on a campaign to rid the town's main street of the A6 traffic. This wasn't achieved until 1970 when the M6 was opened. (*Anon/J. Marsh Collection*)

The main road over the Shap fells gained a notoriety which preceded the advent of the motor vehicle. If there are ghosts in Westmorland following sudden and violent death this view must show the site of their hauntings. The main road seen in the centre of the view is the Heronsyke to Eamont Bridge turnpike which was acquired by the County Council from the Quarter Sessions in 1889. A smaller road on the left of the picture is the very early (medieval or before) road that Bonnie Prince Charlie's army took when retreating from their failed 1745 rebellion. In the stream in the bottom of the valley the Scots army abandoned their cannon which was picked up by their rearguard just before the last battle on English soil at Clifton Moor only a few miles to the north. When the A6 started to take motorised traffic there were many fatal accidents on 'Hucks Brow', the hill in the centre of the picture, and these carried on until the M6 was opened. (*J. Marsh Collection*)

The Huck family, whose name was given to the hill on the A6 over Shap fells lived in the cottages in the background of this photograph, which shows one of the fatal accidents that seemed to happen all too frequently outside their front door. A daughter of the family, Lenore, married into the Knowles family on the nearby Hollowgate farm and became famous locally as the lady who wound the Leyland clock which for some years graced the roadside near Hollowgate. It was Mrs Knowles who kindly supplied me with this picture from her extensive archive of the parish of Selside. (*Anon/L. Knowles*)

Church Street, Ambleside, with an early accident in the days of steam-driven lorries. The steam lorry that hit the cycle shop of Clark and Gibson is seen having its load removed on to a Leyland diesel lorry owned by Ernest Bennett of Ambleside. No details or date come to us with the picture, but it can be presumed that the steering on the steam lorry failed as it turned into Church Street from Lake Road. Note the solid tyres on both vehicles. (*Anon/J. Marsh Collection*)

Langdale in the snow looks an unlikely place and time to go for a ride in an open-top Model T Ford. Braving the elements are members of the Pepper family who claim to have had the first car in Langdale. That family's fame in connection with the Langdale linen industry, started by John Ruskin in the nineteenth century, has been much written about in recent years. (*Pepper family/J. Marsh Collection*)

Windermere on the Kendal road, when Emerson & Hazard's fair vehicles pause for a photograph to be taken. The narrow unmade road can be seen; except for a surface of tarmacadam, it remains much the same today. The Westmorland roads policy was once described as 'Do nowt and take a long time about it'. Four heavily laden trailers behind the Fowler showman's engine 'Lightning 1' were on their way to the next 'fair', possibly at Ulverston or Kendal. (*Herbert of Windermere/G. Dawson Collection*)

Holmescales, Old Hutton, near Kendal, was the scene of camps for volunteer soldiers from all over the north of England in the years leading up to the First World War. The transport for many of these soldiers was the bicycle and it looks as though the men had brought their own machines, as a number of different types of cycle can be seen. The unmade minor road seen in the photograph looks of a similar quality to the main roads of the time. It was not until well after the Second World War that the county council was able to improve the minor roads. (*YMCA/J. Marsh Collection*)

Shap Wells hotel, just off the A6 main road attracted many passing motorists and was also a venue for travellers arriving at Shap railway station. Many came to take the waters, as this was also a 'spa' hotel – with foul tasting water available from a spring in the grounds. The locals said the water tasted of train smoke mixed with bad eggs. During the war this hotel became a camp for captured German officers. The photograph dates from 3 July 1936 when R.J. Clark was the proprietor. (*R.J. Clark/J. Marsh Collection*)

In February 1955 the Kirkby Stephen to Brough road was blocked by heavy snowfalls and the ex-War Department armoured personnel carrier that the county council had acquired and fixed a snow plough to was, like all other traffic, stuck. The roadmen are busy, in these two pictures taken by the author, removing snow so that their snow plough can continue on its way. The children add snowballs to the hazards of the day. (*Above and below: J. Marsh/J. Marsh Collection*)

The Sedbergh road bridge on the main railway line from Oxenholme to the north was interesting until, on electrification, the main beam was replaced and the original, which dated back to and commemorated the original 1846 Lancaster & Carlisle Railway, was removed. It seems a pity that this interesting memorial is now lost, and it is just as well that local train enthusiast and historian Preston Whiteley recorded the beam on 20 October 1962 before its removal by British Rail contractors. (*Preston Whiteley/P. Whiteley Collection*)

Oxenholme Junction was an important Westmorland railway location. It was here that the Windermere railway, completed a few months before the main line over Shap, joined the main line. Originally there were engine sheds here for the locomotives that were needed to help trains over 'the hump', the route north over Shap fells. A small village was built and Kendal acquired a suburb. In this Preston Whiteley picture from July 1963 the junction can clearly be seen on the left with the steam-hauled Liverpool–Glasgow train pulled by 4–6–0 no. 42571. Scenes such as this were, not too many years ago, a common sight but the arrival of diesel engines and then electrification has changed the scene completely. Readers interested in the railways of the county should read *Cumbrian Railways* by the author and John Garbutt (Sutton, 1999) and *Images of Cumbrian Railways* (Sutton, 2002). (*P. Whiteley Collection*)

Windermere railway station. Above we see the long platforms provided to accommodate the very long tourist trains that brought thousands to the village. The right of this picture is now occupied by a large Lakeland Ltd building and its car parks. The picture on the left shows the scene on 13 August 1962, in the height of the season, when a shunting accident sent carriages through the end wall of the station, luckily with no injuries. The reduction of traffic into Windermere station, where tens of thousands used to alight, has resulted in the motor traffic pollution that Windermere and Bowness villages, as well as other places en route, suffer today. (P. Whiteley/P. Whiteley Collection)

The Windermere branch at Oxenholme in steam days is seen in these two photographs. Right, a double-headed train pulls off the Windermere platform at Oxenholme on its way south, headed by Stanier 2–6–4 tank engines 42301 and 42464. Below, the Windermere train from the south pulls down the incline towards Kendal and Windermere with a three coach local headed by Stanier 5MT 4–6–0 no. 44680. This train may have been part of a longer train which split at Oxenholme, with the main part travelling north on the main line. (*N. Stead/N. Stead Collection*)

Shap Summit signal box with Jubilee class 4–6–0 no. 45657 hauling a northbound express, 24 June 1961. It was to locations such as this that young Westmorland people brought their notebooks for trainspotting, which was a widespread pastime. This engine would have been a special as it carried a name, *Tyrwhitt*: named engines were an exciting extra. (*P.B. Booth/N. Stead Collection*)

Opposite: The railway line near Tebay with goods trains. Above, 'Black Five' 4–6–0 no. 45120 rushes over the Dillicar water troughs with a mixed milk and parcels train in the 1950s. The engine is picking up water from the troughs, as can be seen by the spray under the tender wheels. This was a popular spot for Westmorland trainspotters and many spectacular railway pictures have been taken here. Below, a train of goods vans is heading south just south of Tebay Junction station, which can be made out in the background. The engine is an ex-War Department 'Austerity' locomotive, built for the Ministry of Supply during the Second World War and after the war sold to the LNER and later British Rail. These powerful engines were designed for long-distance heavy freight trains and thus made light of haulage over the fells of Westmorland. The local train spotters were well pleased when they recorded one of these monsters in their records. (*N. Stead/N. Stead Collection*)

Ravenstonedale railway station was on the north-eastern line from Tebay to Kirkby Stephen and Darlington, which was originally built to allow coke trains to travel from the industry in the north-east to the steel furnaces of the Furness area. An early guidebook stated that 'The erection of the South Durham Railway put Ravenstonedale in connection with the world outside its own hills'. The line was closed in 1962. Just before closure special trains were run for enthusiasts to enjoy the nostalgia of riding on a soon-to-be-closed railway. Here such an enthusiasts' special is seen at Ravenstonedale station eastbound between Tebay and Kirkby Stephen East. Heading the train is an ex-LNER J21 class 0–6–0 no. 65061, a type of engine which was frequently seen on the west side of Stainmore on passenger trains. Note the 'Northern Dales Rail Tour' headboard. Assisting is ex-LMS Ivatt Mogul class 2–6–0 no. 46478, which was also an engine type commonly seen on Westmorland railways in BR days after the war. The remarkable thing about this station is that it was not in the village of Ravenstonedale but in the adjoining village of Newbiggin on Lune. The station house can still be seen overlooking the new road that was built on the line of the railway after closure. (*N. Stead Collection*)

Opposite: Appleby West station on the Settle–Carlisle Midland Railway line remains in operation today, but these two June 1965 photographs show goods traffic on the line at a time when closure was being considered even though the line was busy. Above, 'Black Five' 4–6–0 no. 44993 hauls a northbound mixed goods towards the station from the south, and below, one of the monsters of steam traction, 2–10–0 9F no. 92055, hauls a 'Long Meg' mineral train south on the same day. Not introduced until 1954, this class of engine had a short life before the end of steam in the 1960s. (*P.B. Booth/N. Stead Collection*)

The main line station at Grayrigg was closed to passengers in 1954 but remained a haunt for Westmorland trainspotters for some time afterwards. The British Railways Board advertised the station buildings for sale for some time but in the end, with no sale, most were demolished. Above, the milk train hauled by Type 4 Diesel electric locomotive no. D212 can be seen pulling through the remains of the station on 7 July 1963, and below, on the same day, the station buildings await their fate nine years after closure. (*P. Whiteley/P. Whiteley Collection*)

Grayrigg station buildings, seen here on 7 July 1963, were typical of the scene all over Westmorland through the decades of railway closures when, even before the famous Dr Beeching, stations were being closed and land and buildings sold off. From Kirkby Lonsdale in the south (see below) to Cliburn in the north of the county the closures and sales were being carried on through the 1950s and 1960s. Kirkby Lonsdale station, which was sited in Lancashire although the town, some miles away, was in Westmorland, closed in 1964 but the buildings survive today. They were sold as a dwelling by British Rail, which could not find a buyer for Grayrigg either. (*P. Whiteley/P. Whiteley Collection*)

Above: Cliburn station was on the same line as Kirkby Stephen East but on the section north of Appleby, which ran to a connection with the North Western main line just south of Penrith. If it was open today it would serve a large holiday complex built in the woods nearby. The line and station closed in 1962 but quarry traffic and the army at Warcop continued to use the track until the 1980s (the quarry traffic finished a couple of decades before the army traffic). It remains to be seen whether Cliburn station with its adjoining holiday camp will reopen as the efforts to open the line in the Appleby area continue. It would be an interesting extension, and might save lives on the dreaded A66 road that serves the holidaymakers now. (*P. Whiteley Collection*)

Left: Kirkby Stephen East station had extensive goods sidings and an engine depot, and was the scene of much round the clock activity when the author lived at Kirkby Stephen in the mid-1950s. It could hardly be envisaged that railway economics were so bad that within a decade the line from the north-east would close and Kirkby Stephen East station, goods yard and depot would be no more. This also meant that handy shopping trips to Darlington and Durham were a thing of the past unless you travelled by car over Stainmore. These buildings still exist, as they were used by a building firm over the decades. Today it is highly likely that the section of rail to Appleby, and maybe beyond, will be reopened as a holiday line, and Kirkby Stephen East station will again see passengers, although for a much reduced service. (*P.B. Booth/N. Stead Collection*)

Gaisgill station (above) on the north-eastern line into Tebay and Sandside (below) are two more railway stations that ceased to exist during the railway cutbacks in the middle of the twentieth century. Passenger traffic ceased to this small rural station in 1952 and the platforms were removed. The line from Tebay to Kirkby Stephen East continued in use as a goods line with the odd non-stopping passenger train until the 1960s. The signal box and signal as well as the level crossing gates have now all gone, but the railway station building remains as a house standing besides the road that was built on the route of the railway following full closure. Below, at Sandside, which at one time (before the building of the railways) was Westmorland's only port – the port of Milnthorpe, which stretched all the way to Arnside – we can see the demolition of the station in hand in February 1966. A contractor's caravan is on the site of a station that at one time was a popular venue for holidaymakers from all over the north. The Hincaster to Arnside line was opened in 1876 for the same reasons as the north-east line over Stainmore, to bring coke to the Furness steelworks. When the trade ceased this branch was closed, in 1963. It is a pity the station was replaced by ugly 1960s-style flats. (*Above and below: P. Whiteley/P. Whiteley Collection*)

Windermere offered a good stretch of water for enthusiasts to experiment with the new craze of flying in the early twentieth century. As can be seen, these new hydro-aeroplanes gave no indication of the future of aviation. Westmorland never got an airport as many counties did, and although plans were put in hand for an aerodrome near Kendal it came to nothing. The lake of Windermere remained the only place where serious flying took place. During the Second World War the lake acquired an adjoining flying boat factory near Troutbeck Bridge, where Shorts built their famous Sunderland flying boats. Above, a biplane (with two wings) is seen, and below, a monoplane (one wing) taxis down the lake. (*Above: Herbert & Son, Windermere/J. Marsh Collection. Below: Anon/J. Marsh Collection*)

Boats at Ambleside in the early years of photography conclude this chapter about Westmorland transport. The county was always a place that more people passed through than lived in, and Windermere was no different with its steamboats, which were introduced on to the lake in 1845, with the intention of providing holidaymakers with a boat trip. The *Dragonfly* paddle steamer was built in 1850 and was one of the first boats to establish the length of the lake trip, which the railway companies took over in later years. The Furness Railway was the main developer of the lake service, which was included in their round the Lake District tours that were advertised all over the UK. The railway line to Newby Bridge at the other end of the lake did not open until 1867 so two paddle steamers, the *Dragonfly* and the *Firefly*, plied the lake before then. The *Firefly*, seen here, appeared after the Kendal to Windermere line was opened by the London & North Western Railway in 1847; it was taken over by the Furness Railway in 1867. The name of the original company which built the *Firefly* remains with us today: when British Rail was being split up and sold, the Windermere lake steamers were acquired by the Windermere Iron Steamboat Company. This picture of a much changed scene at Waterhead, Ambleside, comes to us from the 1850s, but there is no trace of the photographer on the print. Both Garnett of Windermere and Baldry of Grasmere are likely but early photographers from further away such as Payne-Jennings (who can be found elsewhere in this book) came from America, on the trail of the romantic image of the English Lake District put about by the Lake Poets and others. (*Anon/J. Marsh Collection*)

2

Westmorland Meets the Sea

Arnside Tower, on the border of Westmorland with Lancashire, is reputed to have been built in the late fourteenth century by the de Thweng family, and survives today as the best undeveloped example of its type in the county. There was a terrible fire in 1602 but the tower was reoccupied for a short time, before its roof timbers were removed and decay set in at the end of the seventeenth century. The south-west angle was blown down in a high wind, leaving the scene shown by local photographer J.D. Wilson in about 1900. Fortified houses such as this are a reminder of the difficult times experienced in the Barony of Kendal in the medieval period. (*J.D. Wilson/J. Marsh Collection*)

Arnside beach was where many caught themselves their next meal. Both photographs are from about 1910. The one above shows the use that fishermen put their boats to when the summer visitors were in the village. The clinker-built prawners were probably built locally at the Arnside boatbuilders Crossfields and were very stable, so the owners were able to offer safe trips round the bay, which were very popular. The sender of this postcard records how his nephews had been catching dabs or flukes by paddling off the sands. Below, the prawner yachts are off to catch the famous Morecambe Bay shrimps, which were then a very popular food. They were sent by train to markets in Lancashire where potted shrimps were in great demand. Agrichemicals have virtually wiped out this trade in recent decades, as they are swept down the rivers into Morecambe Bay. (*Above and below: J.D. Wilson of Arnside/J. Marsh Collection*)

The Arnside promenade attracted many, who came there by train and coach, unlike today where the scene would show rows of parked motor vehicles. The result of a storm in March 1907 is shown below. Much damage was done to embankments and, of course, the boats at Arnside front. A large prawner yacht is seen pushed up near Crossfields yard where, years before, it had probably been built. Nets and masts can be seen strewn around. So, like any coastal town, Arnside was at the mercy of the weather. (*Above and below: J.D. Wilson of Arnside/J. Marsh Collection*)

The Crown Hotel on Arnside front is still to be seen, but it has reverted to its original name of the Fighting Cocks. It is reputed to date back to the seventeenth century and was the first inn in Arnside. The first MC of the Arnside Regatta was a Mr Titterington, who was landlord of the Fighting Cocks. These regattas were held every summer between 1846 and 1906 with a course from Arnside round Holme Island at Grange-over-Sands. This photograph was taken just after the silted-up bay stopped the yachts sailing to Grange. Passengers from the Furness Railway train in the background are enjoying the hotel's facilities, which included horse carriage trips around local beauty spots, of which there were many. (*J.D. Wilson/J. Marsh Collection*)

Dallam Park at Milnthorpe was where the Kent river had provided a small port for Milnthorpe from at least the middle ages. The port closed when the huge railway bridge for the Hincaster to Arnside Railway line was built across the mouth of the River Bela where it joined the Kent. This fine bridge lasted from its erection in 1876 until, just after the line's closure, it was demolished in 1966. (*Mashiter of Milnthorpe/J. Marsh Collection*)

The knotted larch trees on Arnside Knott indicate a glorious Victorian pun: four larch trees were knotted as saplings to make what became a favourite spot for holidaymakers trudging to the top of the limestone hill overlooking Arnside. Not much of them remains today but they are still sought out by visitors. Writing from Stoneleigh in Arnside in June 1909, on the reverse of this postcard, John writes to Maggie Carruthers that he is 'having a quiet, peaceful, serene and gentle holiday. I wonder how your old boy feels without you?' Arnside was a holiday resort with a few hotels and many B&Bs when the card was sent to Ilkley in Yorkshire. (*J.D. Wilson/J. Marsh Collection*)

Milnthorpe was Westmorland's only port until the arrival of the railway in the mid-nineteenth century. The slow transformation from that time into a run-down town on the national transport system in the mid-twentieth century was hardly planned; it just happened. The top picture is of the Tattersall almshouses completed in 1895 on land given by the Bindloss family. It could hardly have been a haven of rest as the lane outside became the main A6 road, with heavier and heavier lorries grinding up the hill from Milnthorpe centre. Below can be seen the Milnthorpe crossroads. The narrow road entrance on the right was widened by removal of the little shop and adjoining cottage, and the home of the Bindloss family found itself on the corner. The traffic built up year on year throughout the twentieth century, completely ruining the historic small town. (*Above: G. Wilson of Grange-over-Sands/J. Marsh Collection. Below: Matthews of Bradford/J. Marsh Collection*)

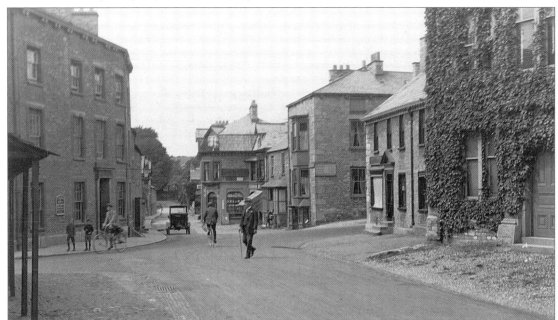

Fairy Steps between Beetham and Sandside was a natural cleft in a limestone cliff that is said to have marked the route to Beetham church. When the road deviated it became a place that people visited through curiosity: it became a 'must-see' for holidaymakers and a place to take a picnic. The picture above shows such a picnic in full swing with a summer crowd. Below is a more peaceful scene with the fairy, probably a daughter of the Atkinson family, neatly posing in costume on the steps. (*Above: G. Howarth of Lancaster/J. Marsh Collection. Below: J. Atkinson of Ulverston/J. Marsh Collection*)

This 'bathing pool for Heversham' school photograph of the 1920s must have caused many a parent to wonder for the safety of their child. Use of the dyke-like River Kent by the school as a swimming pool may seem dangerous to us today, but before the Second World War 'character building' was part of schooldays – until the pupils rebelled after the war. (*Marshall, Keene & Co., Hove/J. Marsh Collection*)

Levens Hall with its famous topiary gardens was just a few miles up the River Kent from the picture above. It is now a major attraction to visitors to south Westmorland. The hall has been continually occupied over many centuries and, with its surrounding deer park that enhances the delightful setting, it is now on national and international itineraries for visits to the Lake District. Generations of owners have served their county well. (*Mashiter of Milnthorpe/J. Marsh Collection*)

Milnthorpe and Levens Hall joining together in the Fair and Radish Feast was the subject chosen by Cynicus, who usually took transport for his theme. (His 'Grange to Kendal and Back in a Day' picture can be found on page 101 of *Cumbrian Railways*, published by Sutton in 1999.) The Mayor of Kendal was called down to open the feast on 12 May with sports, radishes and Morocco ale for the participants. The feast and fair were held annually from the seventeenth century until 1880. (*Cynicus/J. Marsh Collection*)

Meathop is an isolated corner of the coast of Westmorland and it was here in 1891 that a convalescent home was built, which was adopted by Dr W.S. Paget-Tomlinson as the Westmorland Consumption Sanatorium. Dr Paget-Tomlinson of Biggins, Kirkby Lonsdale, is seen here with his groom on the drive to the main building. The site chosen adjoined the site of Grange-over-Sands gasworks: the wealthy inhabitants had chosen a site well out of both the town and the county of Lancashire for their gasworks. The authorities at the time put out the information that gas works fumes were good for the lungs of consumptives. (*Wilson of Grange-over-Sands/J. Marsh Collection*)

Meathop Sanatorium from the air at about the time of the First World War. This photograph shows how the county facility had grown. This is the men's section, and there was also an extensive women's section. The fresh air cabins, which, with gasworks smoke, were part of the treatment, can clearly be seen dotted round the site. For many months people diagnosed with TB rested in these cabins with one open wall. Patients from the north of the county were looked after at the Blencathra Sanatorium near Keswick in Cumberland, where the gasworks' fumes treatment was not included. (*Aero Pictorial, London/J. Marsh Collection*)

Kendal House Farm at Meathop was the southern end of an extensive fruit-growing area which extended down the Lyth valley from Crosthwaite. Photographed in 1917 are two Land Army girls picking fruit, probably damsons, for the farmer James T. Bentham. The Westmorland War Agricultural Committee joined in the national scheme to employ women in farm work as the men had gone off to the front. (*Anon/J. Marsh Collection*)

3

Farming &
Employment

Wharton near Kirkby Stephen, haymaking in a style long dead in the rest of the county,
18 September 1909. The use of a sled to carry the hay to the barn was the ancient method
from the early days of farming the fell lands of Westmorland. Horses and carts elsewhere
replaced the sled method many decades before the picture was taken. Note the man-held sled
on the right. (*Anon/J. Marsh Collection*)

Haymaking at Ambleside (above) and near Low Wood on the Ambleside to Windermere road (below) were both captured by the photographer employed by the Pictorial Stationery Company of London. The holiday business was at its height in about 1900 when these pictures were taken, and many national photographic companies were investing in the requirement for 'wish you were here' postcards. Sold under the trade name of Peacock, these well-posed pictures of Lakeland farming were in great demand by tourists. A barn full of good dry hay ensured a winter without difficulty for most Westmorland farmers and many, with good hayfields, had an income selling their crop to farmers not able to garner enough from their own meagre acres. (*Pictorial Stationery Co./J. Marsh Collection*)

Small fields and backbreaking work in Little Langdale in the 1950s, where men from the Birkett and Hodgson families join in the joint enterprise of bringing in the hay harvest. The pictures show the hay being turned to dry it out and its collection on to an overloaded cart at Birk How Meadow. A perk for the horse was that it was allowed to eat as much of the crop as it could. (*Hodgsons of Wilson Place*)

Opposite, top: The Gardner family of Spout House, Crosthwaite, Lyth valley, are reputed to have raised twenty-two children and so were, for a time, self-sufficient at hay and harvest times. Here three of the daughters join the men in picking up what looks like a bumper crop of hay. (*Greavan of Crosthwaite/the late Mrs Taylor's Collection*)

Above: The small field adjoining the railway station at Burneside near Kendal gave the haymakers odd moments of passing interest as the trains came and went. Here Aaron Sharp and his brother from Garnett House Farm are seen with an overloaded cart so typical of Westmorland. 'Get it in quickly before it rains' must have been the cry. (*Anon/J. Marsh Collection*)

Left: Jesus church, Troutbeck, gives a backdrop to an activity similar to haymaking, when the road lengthman cleared and tidied his roadside as though it was a garden. Over the wall next to the workman was a plot of land used by the County Council to dump roadmaking materials, so often needed on this main road to Kirkstone and Ullswater. (*Stengal, London/J. Marsh Collection*)

Great Strickland in the north of the county, where at Dallam Bank George Thornborrow (with a rake) poses with his family and the farm lad against yet another overloaded hay cart. Related to many farming families in the south of the county, George was a tenant of Lord Lonsdale of Lowther. (*Anon/J. Marsh Collection*)

Burton in Kendal where, in a field overlooking the main street, a farmer introduces his son to the mechanised way of turning hay after cutting. Horse-drawn devices such as this saved much of the back-breaking work shown elsewhere. Mechanisation continued, to such a degree that farmers changed the landscape to accommodate the new machinery, sweeping away hedges, banks and anything that got in the way of what they were doing. (*W. Hoggarth/ J. Marsh Collection*)

Mechanised haymaking, early twentieth-century style. Above, a pause in the cutting of a field of hay at Ambleside is recorded for posterity by Walmsley Bros of Ambleside. Farm machinery was generally not well looked after, and it was common for it to break down as soon as it came into use after sitting rusting away for a year in either a barn or a field corner. The horses found the photographer of more interest than the repair man. Below, Benson Hayton of Plumtree Farm, Crosthwaite, works his lonely way round a hayfield. Cutting hay was once a community activity with the horses only appearing when the grass was taken in. Machinery made the task a lonely activity with only the horses to talk to, and a lot of time to ponder the bank overdraft and other farming problems. Maybe the advent of mechanised farming took a lot of the fun away, but at the same time it took away the backache. (*J. Marsh Collection*)

Millbeck Farm, Natland, Kendal, with Holly Chapman loading the last forkfuls of hay on to a large four-wheeled cart in the 1930s. On many farms back-breaking work continued until the Second World War and after. In Millbeck Farm's case the spread of housing development was to change everything, as the fields were consumed by the spread of the outskirts of Kendal. (*Chapman family/J. Marsh Collection*)

New Road, Kendal, was chosen to display the machinery owned by George Houghton. The Allchin steam traction engine, which not only hauled everything to the farm but also, when there, provided the power for the threshing machine and the 'tier' are posed for a photograph to illustrate an advertisement for the local farming press. Set-ups like this were leading towards the combine harvester, which included its own transport as well as a mechanised system to carry out all parts of a farmer's harvest. (*J.K. Ellwood/G. Dawson Collection*)

The Langdale linen industry founded by John Ruskin of Brantwood, Coniston, had a number of interesting social offshoots. Not only did the Pepper family have an interesting landlady in the shape of Beatrix Potter, who acquired the Holme Ground Estate where they lived, but also Mary Ellen Pepper (1872–1949) was chosen by Sir John Everett Millais as the model for his painting *Cherry Ripe*. Mary Ellen's daughter, Elizabeth Fell, is seen as a child in 1907 and as a schoolgirl at Little Langdale School in about 1914. Holme Ground was just in Lancashire but the nearest Lancashire school was at Coniston, some distance away from Tiberthwaite. Children from that area walked over the fell into Westmorland where there were two schools, one in Little Langdale and the other in Great Langdale. To support the Langdale linen industry the crop to be found on both sides of the Lancashire/Westmorland border was flax or hemp, which was harvested to be made into the cloth used by the industry. (*The Pepper family archive*)

Children became involved in farm life from an early age, as the boys were generally to work in farming and the girls married into farms and farming. Above, we see Crosthwaite children at Guide Post Corner with a hand barrow laden in the haymaking style with the senior girl carrying the refreshments. Maybe a number of the lads would be off to the First World War about five years after this picture was taken. Below, at about the same time, children of the Woof family of Clawthorpe Hall Farm, Burton in Kendal, pose in the field on the Holme Road where the M6 now runs. Related to the Thornburrow family at Great Strickland (see p. 66), this farmer was also a tenant of Lord Lonsdale. (*Above: Greavan of Crosthwaite/the late Mrs Taylor's Collection. Below: Anon/the late Mrs Baker's Collection*)

The Langdale linen industry spread from the initial work undertaken by the Pepper family in Langdale. At Bowness-on-Windermere Annie Garnett set up a business at The Spinnery, which can be seen in the top picture. This was a place much visited as it was in the centre of a busy holiday resort, and it became very popular and well known. Its memory lives on in the Folk Museum at Kendal's Abbot Hall where many relics of this business can be seen. At Troutbeck Bridge on the Windermere to Ambleside road the Cottage Linen Industry, which advertised Greek lace and art needlework, was run by the Misses Dick, who said their shop was a branch of John Ruskin's Cottage Home Industry. Foreign products undercut prices after 1918, but these two businesses struggled on when many had given up. (*Above: Anon/Gill Carrick Collection. Below: Anon/J. Marsh Collection*)

Lyth Valley farmers had ancient peating rights built into the ownership or tenancy of their farm. The rights could be exercised, of course, where the peat was to be found, which was often a long way from the farm. Above, we see the Gardner family from Spout House, Crosthwaite, digging peat on their plot at the beginning of the twentieth century. Note the peating barrow, which permitted a high stack of peats to be carried. Below, a farmer from Brigsteer is pictured with his barrow on top of the baulk. In the days before coal came into general use peat was dug in time to allow a long drying period in summer, before the peats were taken indoors to use as fuel. In Westmorland peat was very popular as it gave off more heat and lasted longer than wood. (*Above: Greavan of Crosthwaite/the late Mrs Taylor's Collection. Below: Anon/J. Marsh Collection*)

This is a famous photograph from the days when peat was one of the main fuels for domestic fires in south Westmorland. Charlie Shaw was a carrier as well as a grocer and keeper of the Bridge Inn. He was given the name of 't' peat fella' in Kendal where he traded cut peats on the streets of the town. The peat was cut out of Levens moss at Whitsuntide each year and, after stacking high to dry out over summer, was sold to keep the fires in local grates burning over winter. It is recorded that eight peats were sold for 1d but there is also recorded the old Kendal cry of 'ten a penny so long as we have any'. Charlie Shaw walked into Kendal with his horse-drawn high-sided cart loaded with peat. He could ride home in his empty cart. (*Anon/J. Marsh Collection*)

Blacksmiths were an important part of every village as they were required to carry out so many different tasks. Above we see Stewardson's smithy at Crosthwaite with two horses having their shoes attended to. Below is the scene at Anthony Nelson's smithy and builder's store at Old Hutton, where a customer could also use the post office facilities at Bridge End, run by the same family. Who needed a newspaper when a visit to Anthony Nelson's with the horse and cart would provide all the free news a farmer would require (and a good gossip about the village goings on as well)? (*Above: Greavan of Crosthwaite/J. Marsh Collection. Below: J. Simcoe of Kendal/J. Marsh Collection*)

Also from Nelson's at Old Hutton comes this picture of 'hooping', or fitting a metal tyre on to a wooden cart wheel. The tyre is in a fire to enlarge it, and then it is knocked on to the wheel while still hot. Careful measurements of radius and circumference of both wood and metal produced a wheel that would last for many years. If it was wrong the tyre dropped off on the first use. Nelson's, being both joiners and wheelwrights as well as blacksmiths, were able to provide all the wheels needed for carts and carriages in the district east of Kendal. (*Anon/J. Marsh Collection*)

Rearing sheep was the main business of most of the Westmorland farms and smallholdings. Above, a nineteenth-century shepherd is seen with a small flock of ewes and lambs in Easdale above Grasmere. Below, sheep shearing at Fell Foot, Langdale, when the family there had the most appropriate fell farmer's name of Mutton. A number of the men to be seen were shearing gang men who toured the farms charging for their skills in removing sheep fleeces quickly and cleanly. A lady of the farm is providing refreshments for all involved, with a daughter and son observing the goings on for future reference. (*Above: Smiths Suitall/J. Marsh Collection. Below: J. Atkinson of Ulverston/J. Marsh Collection*)

Sheep gather at Hills Bottom, Hartley Fold, Kirkby Stephen, in the snow in 1954. The sheep had been brought down, to aid feeding, from the high fell tops and gathered together at Hills Bottom but, as can be seen on the left of the picture, they were pawing the snow off the ground to get at the grass underneath. Loss of animals in a bad winter was a risk all fell farmers understood and tried to avoid. (*J. Marsh/J. Marsh Collection*)

Prize-winning sheep were much sought after at sheep sales, especially if breeding to produce another prizewinner was the intention. The animals were also likely to have both good meat and wool and thus higher value. Here William Richardson of Laverock Bridge poses with his Wensleydale ram/Rough Fell ewe cross which won the Half Bred Shearling Gimmer class at the Kendal Show in September 1909. Even the sheep looked proud of its achievements. (*J. Marsh Collection*)

The Dargue family of Burneside Hall were prizewinners many times in local agricultural shows, and above we see J. Dargue with his prize-winning Blackfaced Scotch ram at Kendal Show in September 1908 when it won first prize in its class. Below we see Mr Dargue again at the same show, where the Blackfaced Scotch ewe won first prize too. The competition in these agricultural shows produced good stock breeding. Attending a show, meeting friends and generally having a good time was also a relief from the hard and dirty work of raising sheep. (*Anon/J. Marsh Collection*)

Kirkby Stephen was the centre of a huge sheep-rearing area and the sheep sales there brought people from a long way away to watch the goings on. The author was at the 'Tup Fair' sales in October 1954 when a Swaledale ram was sold by J.E. Harker and Sons of Murton Hall for the then huge amount of £1,800. Mr Harker is seen here with his prize-winning ram. The purchaser can be seen on p. 45 of *Cumbrian Memories* by J. Garbutt and the author (Sutton, 2000). 'Tha cud a bowt a row of houses with that money', was a local comment at the time. The St Luke fair was held from medieval times in the main street of Kirkby Stephen, but so many complaints about the mess and nuisance left behind were made in the early twentieth century that the sale was moved to the auction mart in Back Lane. How many of the visitors to the tup sales could understand the local dialect, which was almost entirely old Norse, it would be hard to report, but many visitors to auction marts and such sheep sales are known to have gone only to listen to the dialect. With the advent of 'better' education and the input from radio and television this wonderful leftover from over a thousand years ago is gradually disappearing, so that 'Towd yow louping oer't yat' or 'T kinder laking in't beck' will mean nothing to anybody except the Scandinavians before long. (*J. Marsh Collection*)

During the Second World War Wrynose Pass was an unmade track from Dunnerdale into Langdale, and in spite of increasing traffic it was to remain so for some years after the war, until a joint committee of Lancashire, Cumberland and Westmorland County Councils stumped up enough cash to make the track into a road. This is the flock belonging to the Hodgsons of Wilson Place, Little Langdale, coming off its 'heaf' down to the farm in the 1940s. The older sheep knew the way and the sheepdog at the back rounded up the odd strays so that Mr Hodgson could take his photograph, although two of the sheep at the front looked intent on joining him on the bank. (*Hodgsons of Wilson Place*)

Brotherswater with a flock of ewes and lambs, 1940s. Taking the sheep back to their own 'heaf' after lambing was, in those days, a more relaxing affair before the holiday traffic built up to an extent that would make this picture virtually impossible now. The farmer today is as likely as not to join in the traffic with his own vehicle to transport the animals. Note the fine shepherd's crook. (*J. Marsh Collection*)

Mardale used to see an annual shepherds' meet as large as any in the combined counties of Cumberland and Westmorland. The meet was at the Dun Bull Inn on an agreed date, when farmers and shepherds from over a wide area would get together to swap sheep that had strayed into the wrong flock. The recognition was by the use of pop marks on the sheep's fleece and reference to the herd book for the area where all the farmers registered their mark. The day would round off with a 'merry neet' of songs and merrymaking and, in fact, this brought people from over a wide area who had no sheep to swap: they came only for the company and fun. Even today, when stray sheep are returned in the back of a pickup after a telephone call, 'merry neets' live on in corners of Westmorland, but not at the Dun Bull Inn. This no longer exists as the Manchester Corporation water engineers have demolished it to make way for their Mardale dam (see also pp. 136 and 138). (*Anon/J. Marsh Collection*)

Morland Ploughing Association's meetings were also a chance to get together under the guise of work. The 1913 meeting was caught by photographer Jordison of Penrith. A farmer's field was ploughed by competing young farmers, and prizes were awarded for neatness and straightness of the furrows. The family went to the event as well and a good day was had by all. (*Jordison, Penrith/G. Dawson Collection*)

Cattle in Westmorland were described as follows by F.W. Garnett of Windermere in his book *Westmorland Agriculture 1800–1900*: 'At the beginning of the nineteenth century cattle in the north of the county were of the Galloway or Irish type, while those in the southern division were of the longhorned and Galloway breeds.' Most farmers originally did not expect to make much money raising and keeping milk cows so breeding was carried out for the meat trade. Lord Lonsdale was the first to start breeding shorthorn cattle in 1810, and the last record of the showing of a pedigree Westmorland Longhorn bull was at Shap Fair in 1885. Farmers were proud of their herds and a photograph was not out of place. Above we see Flodder Hall in the Lyth valley with their small herd of brown and white calves, and below at The Green, Lambrigg, a group of shorthorns is pictured in about 1900. (*Above and below: Anon/J. Marsh Collection*)

'Horses have never been the strong feature in Westmorland', says F.W. Garnett, 'and the only breed which has persisted is the hardy fell Galloway which is now known as the Fell Pony. They have been bred on the fells and high moors of Westmorland from time out of mind.' Above we see a group of wild fell ponies on High Street in about 1910. At this time the breeding of horses was gradually disappearing on fell farms as the demand was large for heavy horses for work of all sorts. Garnett records up to four fell ponies being harnessed to a plough in the east of the county. Below, two of the larger farm horses can be seen at Grasmere lake pictured by G. Abraham, who constantly attempted to romanticise the dirty hard work of the Lakeland farmer. It is not likely that the farmers who were photographed would share in the proceeds of the postcard and other picture sales. (*Above: Lowe of Patterdale/J. Marsh Collection. Below: G.P. Abraham of Keswick/J. Marsh Collection*)

The woodyard at Staveley is seen in this photograph from about 1910 with, in the foreground, one of the interesting wagons that were used for carting logs from the wood to the yard. This woodyard adjoined a prosperous woodturning business that produced a number of products for home and industry, the most notable being brush handles for the military. Recently the Brockbank family of Staveley have had to change their woodyard and factory into an industrial estate. Note the pillared open-fronted barn in which wet wood was dried out. (*Anon/J. Marsh Collection*)

The servants' registry on Crag Brow, Bowness-on-Windermere, was where people wishing to work in the big houses, the hotels and on the farms could leave their names in the hope of being offered a job. It was a labour exchange used by both employer and employee. 'Fenty' Robinson's shop was also where drapery materials and other cloth could be purchased; during the First World War the cloth included sacking for making sandbags (see p. 90). Robinson's sideline was a collection of old photographs of the Windermere area, which he kept in large albums, and many people visited his shop just to look at these. The Fenty Robinson collection is now kept at the Windermere public library, where it continues to attract visitors wishing to view nineteenth-century Windermere and Bowness photographs. (*Anon/J. Marsh Collection*)

John William Croft's village blacksmith's shop, Grayrigg, 1905. A fine horse is being reshod. A good range of the work carried on at the smithy is seen, and the notice declares 'Shoeing forge, machinery implements and jobbing smith': all that the village and surrounding area could require. (*Sawyers of Kendal/J. Marsh Collection*)

Windermere wine and spirit merchant Thomas Swainson's premises in Cross Street was a busy place when this photograph was taken in about 1905. Founded in 1874, Swainson's business was a side-effect of the expansion of Windermere and Bowness and the opening of many hotels and boarding houses. They advertised as 'Manufacturers of high class minerals and aerated waters, bottlers of beer, stout, cider, lager beer, etc'. (*J. Marsh Collection*)

The large granite quarries on Shap Fell sold granite in many forms and colours for use all over the world. This advertising photograph of about 1900 shows work in hand breaking up large slabs of rock brought down from the quarry face by explosives. The telegraph address was shown as 'Felspar, Shap' and a note added that 'deliveries are subject to conditions of weather, wagon supply, unforeseen circumstances, Strikes, Lock-outs, Acts of God that may limit or stop production'. In spite of these dire warnings the quarries prospered and had their own railway siding from the London & North Western Railway main line that ran near the quarries. (*Shap Granite Co./J. Marsh Collection*)

Langdale's Thrang Quarry was the source of the world-famous Langdale green slate which was used on roof tops at home and abroad. The quarry men lived in both north Lancashire and Westmorland, as the slate was worked in quarries in the Coniston fells as well as in Langdale. The rows of cottages built for the workers in the quarries by the quarry owners now bring large prices on the open market as holiday homes, a system which drives many of the early twentieth-century quarryworkers' grandchildren out of the area in order to find housing they can afford. (*Raphael Tuck/J. Marsh Collection*)

Thrang Quarry, Langdale, with highly skilled ropework being demonstrated by quarrymen who are clearing the face of loose slabs after an explosion has brought down rock for working into slate. The same type of ropework was used when the face was being drilled to put in explosives. (*Raphael Tuck/ J. Marsh Collection*)

The itinerant photographers who toured county areas taking pictures of schoolchildren also took photographs at any location where a group could be gathered together, and these are Langdale quarrymen. The quarrymen wanted a picture to frame at home and the photographer got many sales from the same picture. These groups are obviously from different departments at the same quarry, but we can only guess the work they undertook. (*Anon/J. Marsh Collection*)

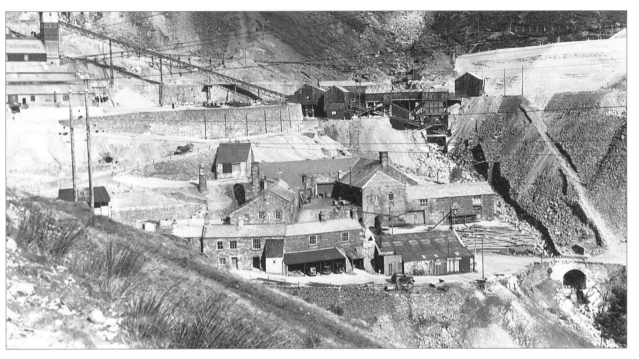

Greenside Lead Mine above Patterdale village provided an output of very high grade lead and other minerals, and employment for many workers who lived in the cottages that can still be seen in Patterdale village today. It also polluted the beck, which ran off the side of Helvelyn into Ullswater, with lead residue. Wordsworth's daffodils danced in the breeze alongside a polluted lake: it may have come to the notice of a Victorian visitor that fishing in Ullswater was not recommended. The mine was closed in 1962 after use by the military to test detection devices for nuclear explosions. Much of what can be seen here has been cleared away but the road over the bridge is still in use, now mostly by holidaymakers en route to the high fells. (*Anon/J. Marsh Collection*)

Lowther Park gates, Eamont Bridge, *c.* 1895, photographed by London photographer Stengal. The picture shows estate workers' children with a doll's pram, and obviously turned out in their best for the picture. It is unfortunate that this lodge and gates were built in the nineteenth century on the site of a henge monument from ancient times, which was part of a larger ancient site now called King Arthur's round table. During the Second World War these gates saw much coming and going of tanks and soldiers engaged in highly secret experiments in Lowther Park, which involved the use of tank-mounted searchlights. Winston Churchill was known to have visited, but whether it was the tanks or the Lowther hospitality that drew him there is not recorded. (*Stengal/J. Marsh Collection*)

Burneside Paper Mill still prospers today and employs many from the area. Mills on the River Kent date back to the twelfth century, although most were then corn mills. Paper mills came to the Burneside area in the eighteenth century mainly through the enterprises of Quaker families who brought the skills of papermaking from elsewhere. The mill was connected to the nearby London & North Western Railway lines. Nearby mills at Cowan Head were also connected by railway. Most of the village of Burneside, its school and its church owe their existence to the Burneside Paper Mill's owners, the present being the Cropper family who acquired the mills in 1845. The photograph dates from 1904. (*Anon/J. Marsh Collection*)

Crag Brow, Bowness-on-Windermere, during the First World War when Fenty Robinson bought in materials to make sandbags for the 'Sandbags for the Front' campaign and also, as the sign in the middle of the picture declares, 'Khaki shirting for our soldiers'. There was probably not much difference in the quality of the materials. The exact financial arrangement for the provision of sandbags and shirts is not known, and must remain a trade secret. Mr Robinson's shop in different days can be seen on p. 84. (*Brockbank of Windermere/J. Marsh Collection*)

Witherslack Mill was typical of many Westmorland watermills. It took its water from the local stream by way of a dam and leat, and was run by the miller and his family who lived nearby. The local farmers brought in their corn for grinding under the large mill wheels and the flour produced was sold by the farmer at market or to millers and bakers. The village mill system was introduced by the Norman barons who did not permit the use of hand mills and ordered that the Lord's mill or a mill licensed by the Lord should be used. This was a form of Norman taxation on people's staple diet: flour and bread. Thomas Dickinson and William Askew were the millers when this photograph was taken in the early twentieth century. (*Wilson of Grange-over-Sands/ J. Marsh Collection*)

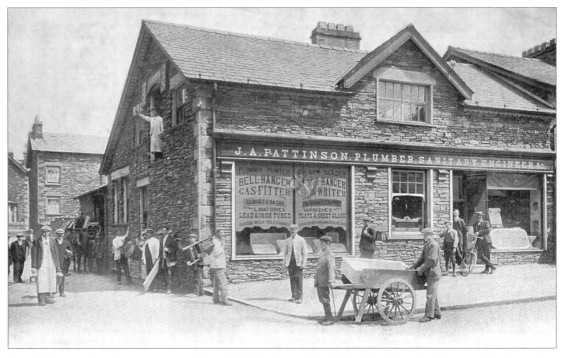

Broad Street, Windermere, was where J.A. Pattinson had his plumbing business and where this photograph was taken to use as a business card. What must have been all his staff are posed round the building. In this case the message on the card told Mr B. Pattinson of Longmire that he could send a cart as his pipes were ready. It was posted on 13 November 1911. (*Anon/J. Marsh Collection*)

Elterwater Extra Special Gunpowder is advertised on the boxes shown in this picture of some of the staff at the Elterwater Gunpowder Works in Great Langdale. Three sticks of the gunpowder can be seen on top of the boxes. The Gunpowder Works was opened by the Huddlestone family in 1824 but was taken over by the Nobel Group (later ICI) in 1918. The photograph comes from the early days of the enterprise. On closure the site was transformed into a holiday camp, with the huts in which the explosives had been mixed being made into sleeping lodges. Much modernised, the site remains in the holiday industry today. (*M. Davies of Millom/Mrs Hodgson, Langdale Collection*)

Estate workers on the Underley estate at Kirkby Lonsdale in the far south of the county were part of a huge number of employees on Westmorland estates. Many would have houses provided by their employer within a short distance of the estate, if not on it. In some cases small villages were built which provided accommodation just for estate workers. Lowther New Town in the north of Westmorland is a good example of this. The woodcutters at Underley were photographed during their tea break with a huge tree awaiting felling after its bark had been stripped. (*Anon/J. Marsh Collection*)

Appleby on market day with the farmers' carriages neatly drawn up awaiting the return of their owners, *c.* 1912. The farmers are gathered in the background around the market hall and moot hall. Appleby was the county town of Westmorland, where the county assize court was held. Market day was Saturday. Until the arrival of the 1880s County Council, Appleby was the centre of local government, police and courts for the whole of the north of Westmorland. The town is a Royal Borough dating from the twelfth century, which status precedes that of Kendal (see later) by some 400 years. (*Anon/J. Marsh Collection*)

Cowper House, Selside, in April 1941, after a disaster caused by a German bomber unloading its bombs miles away from its target of Barrow-in-Furness. James Wood and his wife and mother, his son Joseph and daughter Jean, were all killed, as well as six evacuees who had been brought to the country from the north-east to avoid the bombing and shelling of their home area. This was the only war-time damage caused by the enemy in the county. (*Anon/L. Knowles Collection*)

Selside in happier times. The picture shows Chaplows of Kendal's threshing outfit at work at Selside Hall Farm, then occupied by Mr W. Parkin. The provision of capital equipment by contractors helped Westmorland farmers in their yearly round and also provided groups of specialists employed by the contractors, such as Chaplows, who provided equipment for use all over the south of the county, even to the County Council when required. (*Anon/E. Duckett, Holme Collection*)

Scroggs Lane, Helsington, was where Chaplows, who had their yard nearby, ran a sawmill, one of their small traction engines providing the power when not in use on farm contract. Such an enterprise provided a good service to loggers and joiners, as well as employing both men and equipment at quiet times. (*Anon/J. Marsh Collection*)

Kendal House Farm at Meathop had a fruit harvest that provided an extra income. On p. 60 First World War land girls can be seen helping with the fruit harvest, and here in 1921 the Bentham family is pictured with baskets of damsons, which would be sold in Kendal and other markets in the area. (*Anon/J. Marsh Collection*)

An Ambleside gardener was photographed by Herbert Bell of Ambleside, one of the Lake District's greatest photographers. Coming from a family of chemists, Bell's pictures are always chemically perfect and can be found today in the condition they were in when taken 100 years ago. This fine character study is typical of Bell's work, much of which is preserved today in the Armitt Library in Ambleside, which Bell himself helped to found in 1912 and where he acted as curator for many years. Herbert Bell was also much concerned in the preservation of Wordsworth's Dove Cottage at Grasmere, which is now a world-famous Wordsworth Museum. (*H. Bell/J. Marsh Collection*)

4
Sports, Gatherings & Other Events

The Temple Sowerby Rose Queen on 2 June 1910 was Kate Pearson. The May Day festivities had been restored to the village only two years before after a lapse of twenty-four years, when Lord Hothfield of Appleby Castle presented the village with a 75 ft high maypole which still graces the side of the A66 road today, its use made impossible by the heavy traffic on the road through the village. The *Cumberland and North Westmorland Herald* recorded in 1910 that 'the fete takes the form of a costume procession, maypole and morris dancers and a programme of sports finishing with a dance in the evening'. Numerous decorated carts, cycles and dancing groups were all part of the parade, which started at 2pm headed by two marshals, Dr Stevenson and Mr Hastings, dressed as deputy lieutenants, with the Culgaith Brass Band, a detachment of the Cumberland and Westmorland Yeomanry and some boy scouts. As this book was being written it was announced that Temple Sowerby is to be relieved of its traffic pollution. A bypass has been approved by the government, after the village was voted the worst site for vehicle pollution in the country. The next few years should see the village return to some sort of peace, and maybe the Rose Queen will visit Lord Hothfield's maypole again in safety. (*Anon/J. Marsh Collection*)

Temple Sowerby green, with a dancing group with hoops all ready to join in a May Queen procession before the First World War. It is unfortunate that the date was not included with the picture, which is on a postcard from Ella Lamb to her sister at Warcop asking how mother was keeping. This was in the days before telephones when a postcard could be sent to announce arrival the same day. (*Reed of Penrith/J. Marsh Collection*)

Brough also had village parades for many events. This was for the 1935 Jubilee when a small motor car was decorated with Union flags and occupied by a parade queen and her companions. The A66 traffic would ensure the end of any attempts to have such celebrations after the Second World War. (*Fearnside of Penrith/J. Marsh Collection*)

Kirkby Stephen May Queen in a year before the First World War when the spring weather was a continuation of winter. Smiles are difficult when the body is nearly frozen. This photograph carries the information 'When KS had a May Queen and Maypole (all arranged by J.C. Parkinson) before the 1914 war. The May Queen was Miss Rachel Smith, a pupil teacher at this school.' The photograph was taken at Hills Bottom field, the scene of many of Kirkby Stephen's festivities. (*Anon/J. Marsh Collection*)

Windermere had a rather more serious May procession on 20 May 1910 when a memorial parade for King Edward VII was held. The sun shone and the soldiers looked very smart. Local parades marked many national events with some style. They are not seen very often in the county nowadays. (*Anon/Mrs G. Carrick Collection*)

Ambleside rushbearing parade started in the dim mists of the past when the floor of the church, just rock and soil, had its mat of rushes replaced. The event proved so popular that it was continued into modern times, even though the church floor no longer required a covering. As the village has a major traffic problem, and as the rushbearing is held in July at the height of the holiday season, the event has continued with some difficulty. Above, the procession is seen in the Market Place, *c*. 1900, and below, the 1909 procession passes the Riggs coaching office opposite the Queen's Hotel. (*Anon/J. Marsh Collection*)

The Grasmere rushbearing, 1905. The six girls in green and white tunics hold the ceremonial linen sheet spun in 1891 by the ladies of the Langdale Linen Industry, founded by John Ruskin and Canon Rawnsley. The Grasmere rushbearing is now so much of the Lake District's annual calendar for visitors that it draws thousands and has developed a style of its own. (*Anon/J. Marsh Collection*)

The Coronation parade on 22 June 1911 at Windermere really brought out the crowds, as can be seen in this picture of the local Sea Scouts heading the parade into the village from the railway station. The Sea Scouts had been founded in Windermere in 1905 by J.M. Sladen, a local friend of Sir Robert Baden-Powell, who was the founder of the Boy Scout movement. The press report of this event records that the parade was led by the town band and included the police, Justices of the Peace, UDC councillors, schoolchildren, territorials, fire brigade, friendly societies, postmen, decorated floats and 'private residents'. It was a windy day and two special marquees were blown down, but in spite of this Miss Ullock presented medals to the children. (*Brockbank of Windermere/J. Marsh Collection*)

Maypole dancing was taught in many Westmorland schools and demonstrated at local events. Above, Ambleside schoolchildren are in Borrans Park dancing in aid of the County Hospital in about 1910. The foundation of a county hospital in Kendal as a charity gave the whole of Westmorland the opportunity to hold parades and events to raise money, and most took the opportunity to have a good time in those years before the foundation of the NHS. Even then Friends of the County Hospital continued with events to buy equipment, which ensured the continuation of social gatherings that might easily have died. Below, in the south of the county the Beetham children were photographed as their pole was almost fully plaited with ribbons. Details of the event were not recorded on the photograph. (*Above: Anon/J. Marsh Collection. Below: Mrs Sutcliffe of Burton in Kendal/J. Marsh Collection*)

The Witherslack May Queen in about 1910 was May Thornbarrow of Halecat Cottage, who obviously took the role very seriously. The event was organised by the local school, which required its pupils to pay for their education by providing a load of fuel yearly. As most local families had their own peat diggings this was not a problem. Dr Barwick's charity paid for any who could not provide the fuel. Witherslack School was very much under the influence of Mrs Argles of Eversley and her sister Mary Wakefield, so there would no doubt have been much music. Mrs Argles used to visit in order to lecture on 'the meaning of Empire' on each Empire Day. (*Anon/J. Marsh Collection*)

Windermere Coronation parade in June 1911 is also featured on p. 101. Above, the parade, headed by the town band and local councillors in full formal dress, can be seen coming down Crag Brow. The crowds are smaller but the flags are everywhere. Below, the procession is seen in Lake Road with schoolchildren carrying many flags. The parade ended on The Glebe. (*Above: Brockbank of Windermere/ J. Marsh Collection. Below: Anon/J. Marsh Collection*)

Burton in Kendal Whit Wednesday walk started from the parish church and went to Heronskye field where games were enjoyed. This 1905 procession is seen on Church Bank and is headed by the Burton Band of Hope banner. All the village took part in one way or another, and for many years a decorated cycle parade was included. (*Rowbotham of Burton/J. Marsh Collection*)

Levens' 'Pastoral Play' on 7 August 1909 was *Diana's Vengeance*. The cast posed for their photograph, not looking too happy about the event. Was it too late in the year for a pastoral play? (*Crosland of Arnside/J. Marsh Collection*)

Tebay's annual flower service is seen in July 1906 with the small town band leading the way and the Tebay Band of Hope banner apparently the only flag or banner in the procession. In the north of the county the temperance movement took every opportunity to advertise their presence and to warn of the evils of the demon drink. Tebay, being a railway village, had railway company restraints on its employees which would, to a degree, be a stronger influence towards sobriety; although, as today, the weaker characters would give in to temptation. (*Anon/G. Dawson Collection*)

Burton in Kendal parades tended to gather for a photograph in The Square. One of the village photographers would picture the event so that all participating could have a picture for their memories. This is the Coronation parade for George V in 1911, with the church banner, the Band of Hope temperance banner and the Sedgwick School of Music banner prominent. The influence of Mary Wakefield and Mrs Argles was great in south Westmorland, with church choirs competing in the choir competitions run at Sedgwick House by the Wakefields. (*Rowbotham of Burton/J. Marsh Collection*)

The church fete at Crosscrake also included a decorated cycle parade, with hats and long hair much on display. The photograph is from a set taken by Ashworths of Kendal in about 1905 and was taken in the grounds of Sellet Lodge, the vicarage when the Revd Edward Bannerman was Vicar. (*Ashworth of Kendal/J. Marsh Collection*)

The Windermere Coronation procession of 1911 also included a decorated float competition, and this picture shows the first prize winner with his decorated pony and cart. Three of the children to be seen are his own. The float was 'Of the Four Nations' – England, Ireland, Scotland and Wales, a typical subject in those nationalistic days. (*Brockbank of Windermere/J. Marsh Collection*)

Little Langdale where, above, the Eskdale Foxhounds are being led over the ford at New Houses by huntsman Arthur Irving with local farmers George Birkett and Jim Hodgson, and a group of visitors anxious to see the way that pest control in the valley was carried on. One hunt pack wasn't always used, and below can be seen the Ennerdale and the Eskdale Foxhounds together at the back of the Tourist Rest Inn (now the Three Shires). The combined pack was led by William Porter, the huntsman. Fox hunting in the Lake District using hounds had been developed as an efficient way of pest control over many years, and it is doubtful if any safer efficient system can be used. Fox hunting is a hard, dirty way of passing a day and did not attract much attention from the leisured classes, with the farmers participating only to ensure that foxes were cleared away from their flocks of sheep. (*Hodgson of Langdale/J. Marsh Collection*)

Dallam Tower estate at Milnthorpe had a large set of kennels and a huntsman for quite a different sort of hunting. The Dallam otterhounds ranged over the whole of South Westmorland and elsewhere, and were run to provide a good day out for the followers of such things. The otter population of the rivers and becks of the district was hunted by the local farmers, and it soon became obvious that the Dallam pack was not needed. Here, in about 1910, the Dallam Otterhounds can be seen at Crosthwaite near the church and pub. Maurice Bromley-Wilson of Dallam can be seen with his huntsmen. (*Greavan of Crosthwaite/J. Marsh Collection*)

Patterdale with the Ullswater foxhounds, 20 March 1907. Huntsman Joe Bowman is leading the hunt, which was advertised 'Meet 10am at Patterdale Hotel for Place Fell'. The postcard was sent by Joe Sisson to a Miss Ross in London and says: 'See Turk coupled on the right and Trimmer in centre.' Quite a large crowd had been attracted, but the serious work of clearing the pests off the fell would only be carried out by a few as the going got tough. (*Anon/J. Marsh Collection*)

Brough Hill Horse Fair dates back to very ancient times and is an amazing survivor, as many similar horse fairs have ceased to exist over the centuries. The Appleby Fair also became a gathering of the gypsy and potter families from a wide area, and it is probable that this has kept the fair alive. Even today the Westmorland roads fill with numerous hoop-top caravans and groups of horses on their way to Appleby, although nowadays many families travel by car or van. Above, we see the scene in about 1900 on the fair hill, and below, the scene is in Kirkby Stephen Market Street in the 1960s when a group of these horses and their owner on their way to Appleby took over the centre of that small town. (*Above: Valentine of Dundee/G. Dawson Collection. Below: D.M. Williams/J. Marsh Collection*)

Ambleside Sports is a gathering with its roots in past times that survives into our days. Above, a small turnout for the junior fancy dress competition in the 1920s. The only male entry stands alone in the background dressed as a tramp. For the participants it was altogether a serious affair. Below, for the boys in the same year practice in Cumberland and Westmorland wrestling with Narelli's and Gusselli's ice cream carts close by was a better prospect. The ice cream carts were Model T Ford conversions, and as the weather was fine, for a change, business would be good. (*Above and below: Anon/J. Marsh Collection*)

The start of the Guides Race at Ambleside Sports before the First World War points to the origins of the Sports itself. The Mountain Guides, local lads who hired themselves out to the visitors, started to hold competitions for speed over a set course, and other events were added. A group of youthful guides, with their girlfriends and parents looking on, wait for the race marshals to give the off. (*Anon/J. Marsh Collection*)

Grasmere Sports became world famous and attracted huge crowds. It all started as a wrestling competition on the green outside the Red Lion Inn on the evening of the rushbearing, and this event was transformed in 1852 by a small committee into the modern Sports. Many of the local rich and famous either participated when young or became associated with the running of the Grasmere Sports. Here, in an early aerial photograph, the Sports are photographed by Abrahams of Keswick. (*J. Marsh Collection*)

Grasmere Sports in the early days, photographed by the first official photographer to the Sports, William Baldry, who was for many years the Grasmere schoolmaster and who started and trained many of the famous early twentieth-century Lakeland photographers. Above, a general view of the sports in the 1880s, and below, in 1888, the famous wrestlers G. Steadman and G. Lowden battle it out in Cumberland and Westmorland style. This activity probably came to the area with the Hiberno-Norse Vikings who settled in the Lake District. The Steadman cups and other awards, presented over many years while he was a champion in this sport, can be seen at the Museum of Lakeland Life, Abbot Hall, Kendal. (*Above and below: W. Baldry/J. Marsh Collection*)

Ambleside hockey team, 1905/6 season. A member on the left of the back row looks as though he has been hit on the head. On 5 October 1905 this team, minus its three best players, beat Kendal on the Borrans Field 4–0. Dr Johnston from the local practice of Augustus Johnston and Son at Gale House is reported to have held Ambleside's goal well. (*Anon/J. Marsh Collection*)

Shap cricket – marrieds versus singles – in 1909. The *Mid Cumberland and North Westmorland Herald* recorded how the Shap village cricket team had collapsed in 1909 from being the local league leaders to thirteenth out of twenty-five. They also recorded that a heifer ate a Culgaith player's braces during one match. It is not surprising Shap cricketers had taken to playing among themselves. (*Anon/J. Marsh Collection*)

Pooley Bridge football team in very serious mood, just before the First World War. Reports of matches in the local leagues of both Association and Rugby football were to be found in the local newspapers of the time, and attracted many readers in the days before radio and television. (*Anon/J. Marsh Collection*)

The Gateback Association football team, 1912/13 season. The next season was to be the last until 1919/20, after the First World War, when the club had to be completely reorganised. It was at Gateback that a football referee complained to a spectator about his language, to be told in reply to shut up or get off the man's field. (*Platt of Kendal/J. Marsh Collection*)

The Langdale Association football club were shield winners in the season 1908/9 and here pose proudly with the shield in the school yard. Sport competitions between individual teams and county teams in various leagues were serious affairs, binding villagers and county players and spectators in close-knit communities. (*Anon/J. Marsh Collection*)

Crosthwaite agricultural show, about the time of the First World War. It included Cumberland and Westmorland wrestling in the day's events as well as a competition for the best dressed wrestler, with wives and mothers providing decoration for shorts and long johns, the traditional garb; although in the picture at least two of the men are in their shorts only. (*Greavan of Crosthwaite/the late Mrs Taylor's Collection*)

Arnside Brownies at a camp on Milnthorpe sands, 1920s. Scouts, Guides, Cubs and Brownie groups were to be found in most areas of the county in the pre-war years and there was a great demand for places in all of them. It was fortunate that one of the Brownie leaders included a donkey in the camp provisions, and the girls are here seen enjoying the ride with a small queue waiting their turn. (*Anon/J. Marsh Collection*)

Longmarton with a fell-walking group hiding from the snow in the middle of May 1905. 'Waiting for the snow shower to pass over – we had lunch here', says the postcard. The top of the county had a long-held reputation for weather that consisted of six months of winter and six months of bad weather. (*Anon/J. Marsh Collection*)

Warcop and Musgrave also had annual rushbearing ceremonies which were quite as serious as the more famous Grasmere affair. Above, the band and the children pose in front of Warcop Hall, which was the venue for most of the festivities, after a service in the church. 'A monster tea party is held in the afternoon and the remainder of the day is spent in dancing and other innocent amusements' says a nineteenth-century newspaper report. Below, the Musgrave rushbearing, seen here at about the same time, was an annual event on the feast day of the patron saint of charcoal burners, St Theobald. The first Saturday in July was allocated, as the saint's day is 1 July. A newspaper report of the time read: 'After the children are regaled with tea, buns etc., presents are distributed amongst them, and the evening is spent in dancing by parents and friends.' (*J. Marsh Collection*)

The Kendal annual Rose Queen ceremony in full swing on land where the Castle Grove housing estate is today. The queen was Connie Milburn and the year 1931. The dais with the throne was topped with a large K surrounded by Union flags to emphasise the loyalty of the borough. A large crowd had gathered to view the event. (*Anon/J. Marsh Collection*)

Appleby, 16 June 1910, when the Band of Hope demonstration to emphasise the importance of signing the pledge against the demon drink drew in crowds from the surrounding villages. The banners from Brough and Hoff are obvious in the photograph but banners from at least six other villages can be glimpsed. A few of the ceremonial teacups which were distributed among the children at such gatherings can be seen. The same cups now bring many pounds in antique shops, whereas they cost pennies originally. (*Anon/J. Marsh Collection*)

The Brough Boys Temperance Band comes from an age very different to ours, when alcopop is sold to children in some village shops. This group of young hopefuls would lead the parade in many villages in north Westmorland where the temperance movement was strong, aided by the many Nonconformist churches in the area. Below, the Kirkby Thore Band of Hope parade where today the A66 road pollutes everything. Which is worse, the demon drink or heavy goods lorries? It's the latter that has ruined the tiny village of Kirkby Thore, and made it impossible for a party of children and their leaders to pose for such a group picture. (*Anon/J. Marsh Collection*)

The Penrith Boy Scouts had their Easter camp in Patterdale on Good Friday in 1911. This group photograph was taken home as a memento by many of the participants. The First World War was only three years away, and one wonders how many of these Scouts were drawn into the hell in France and elsewhere, never to return. Baden-Powell, having experienced the awfulness of war, stressed that his Scout movement was not training young men to participate in war, but in 1914 Lord Lonsdale was ranting in the newspapers and on posters 'Are you a man or a mouse?', and many young Cumbrians went to their death as a result. (*Anon/J. Marsh Collection*)

Shap, where the ruins of the Girls' Friendly Society camp can still be seen in the roadside quarry just north of the village. As the traffic increased on the A6, indicated by the line of telegraph posts in the background, the popularity of this annual camp decreased because of the noise and pollution. In this 1930s picture a group of senior Girl Guides from the Furness area have obviously made friends with other girls using the camp. (*Anon/J. Marsh Collection*)

Hard winters had different effects in different parts of the county. Above, the 1929 great freeze brought skaters out on to Windermere lake, and hotels and boarding houses opened their doors in the closed season to cater for the visitors that this huge frozen lake attracted. In the background the Old England Hotel at Bowness looks as though it has not yet caught on to the money-making opportunities being presented by the frost. Below, a 'summer' camp at Appleby in 1906 is hit by snow. 'Dear Mary', says the message on the postcard, 'This is another view taken during the snowstorm. The horse which you see the man has hold of had dropped down with the cold and they had just got it up again when the camera snapped it.' The postcard was dated 26 May. See p. 117 (lower picture) for an illustration of the bad weather in 1905. (*Above and below: J. Marsh Collection*)

The Burton & Holme Boys Rifle Corps was an example of why Baden-Powell founded the Boy Scouts. The Church Lads Brigade and other church youth groups were moved in the direction of military training by leaders who should have known better. Here the Burton & Holme boys pose with their twelve rifles in what looks like their Boys Brigade uniforms: training for the madness of the First World War. (*Mrs Sutcliffe of Burton/J. Marsh Collection*)

Ambleside, where in each of the years leading up to the First World War young men in university officer training units were assembled in a camp on the site of the Roman fort of Galava. Here the 1909 camp is seen in what must have been a warm summer, with the mess tent walls raised. The postcard was sent in August 1909 to Caversham in Oxfordshire, attesting to the geographical spread of the participants. (*Anon/G. Dawson Collection*)

Farleton near Preston Patrick, in the south of the county, was where volunteer camps were held in the summers before the First World War. Above, the transport section of the Liverpool Scottish can be seen in their 1911 camp, with their officers in kilts. Below is a general view of the camp when it became known as the territorials camp. The northern section of the Lancaster to Kendal canal can be seen on a section that has been cut off by the building of the M6, which now runs where the back row of tents are. (*Above: H. Lang of Cardiff/J. Marsh Collection. Below: Anon/ J. Marsh Collection*)

Military camps were all over the county pre-First World War. Above, the scene is in Lowther Park on the northern boundary of Westmorland. Below, the picture is of the huge camp at Homescales near Endmoor in 1911. The neat lines of tents covered large areas of land as volunteer army units were trained for the horrors to come. (*Above: Anon/J. Marsh Collection. Below: YMCA/J. Marsh Collection*)

'Kirkby Stephen Territorials leaving home for service in India, 19 October 1914' is the title of this photograph. It included a joke for those in the know. The lieutenant in charge of the unit was 'Sonny' Highett. He is not occupying the chair in the middle of the group, but has placed his 'sonny' with a drum in his place; it is not known if the other two children shown are also Lt Highett's. Soldiers sent on postings such as this were to replace regular army units on the North-West Frontier, who were being sent into France. (*Anon/J. Marsh Collection*)

Grasmere, 1922, when a troop of Norwegian Sea Scouts, on a holiday trip to visit the Windermere Sea Scouts, were picked up by Mr J.M. Sladen's cars after a day in the lakes. Mr Sladen of Cleeve Howe, Windermere, was a friend of Robert Baden-Powell, who made a number of trips to Westmorland as a result. The Kendal Scout company was called 'Lady Bagot's Own' and was of great interest to Sir Robert, who encouraged other wealthier county families in Westmorland to found Scout groups in their areas. The international appeal of the Scout movement after the First World War was strengthened by the visit to Windermere of the Norwegian scouts from 13 to 29 August 1922. (*Anon/J. Marsh Collection*)

St Mary's School, Windermere, had a Sunday School concert on 24 and 25 April 1908, and this photograph from the archive of Mr Dobson of Troutbeck Bridge shows one of his neighbours, Mr Bill Aspinall, sitting in the chair as a child. There is an obvious Chinese influence on the Windermere children of the time; it is likely that Gilbert & Sullivan's *Mikado*, which was then just twenty years old, was at the root of this. (*Anon/E. Dobson Collection*)

Staveley fire volunteers practise, *c.* 1900. The picture shows the value of being on the voluntary brigade, where the young men of the village get together for the communal good. Practice night would have its problems as the pump and its accessories wouldn't necessarily work. A rather dried-up river bed shows a possible lack of water. In villages such as Staveley the hand pump was provided by one of the local industries. If there was a serious fire outside the village a number of pumps from nearby villages would be called out to tackle the blaze. Our modern fire services date only from the time of the Second World War, and the National Fire Service was split into county brigades in the late 1940s. (*Anon/J. Marsh Collection*)

Kirkby Stephen Red Cross nurses pose for a photograph as they restock their wartime supplies, 12 March 1944. The county medical officer of health had responsibilities in wartime that were passed to volunteer organisations, which were run by trained nurses. Many a district nurse spent her off-duty hours working with the Red Cross nurses as a matter of duty – behaviour that many in our times would find it difficult to explain. (*Anon/J. Marsh Collection*)

The Kirkby Stephen St Luke Fair, 27 October 1911. Sheep were in pens on both sides of the road and a crowd with the town band were in the middle. The social importance of these fair days throughout Westmorland cannot be overstated. The effect on the farming community was tremendous in the days when farmers generally worked on their own. To have social contact with their fellow farmers, and the opportunity to mull over problems and news, was most important. See p. 79 for more on the 'tup sales'. (*Anon/J. Marsh Collection*)

Appleby gatherings are shown here. Above, the Appleby Assize Court, with the judge's arrival being watched by a crowd of onlookers on 6 July 1921. In those days the Judge of Assize could sentence a prisoner to death by hanging; thus the judges were held in awe and a peep at the very important person was something to talk about. The prison and the yard where the very few hangings had taken place were behind the court house, which is in the centre of the picture. Below, a very different scene: the potters and gypsies gather by the River Eden on 'the Sands' to wash their animals and show off riding bareback in the river. The Assize Court is no more, having ceased in 1970, but, unfortunately for the peace of Appleby, the potters and their horses continue, aided by Westmorland romantics, of which there are many. (*Above and below: Whitehead of Appleby/G. Dawson Collection*)

Brougham Hall, and the royal visit that caused much chatter among the populace of north Westmorland and over the river in the Penrith area of Cumberland. The King had arrived without his wife Queen Alexandra, but with his mistress Mrs Alice Keppel, who can be seen in the photograph looking over his left shoulder. More about this visit can be found in *Eden Valley Westmorland* by the author (Sutton, 1992) and *Cumbrian Memories* by the author and John Garbutt (Sutton, 2000). The King had arrived in October 1912 at a time of great political upheaval, which led to the First World War. (*Fearnside of Penrith/J. Marsh Collection*)

On the boundary with Cumberland on the summit ridge of Helvellyn, in 1891, a group of people gathered to erect a cairn to an unfortunate Kendalian who had perished on this spot in 1805. William Wordsworth had perpetuated the memory of the event when he penned his poem 'Fidelity'. This was the tale of the dead man's dog, which had guarded the body for three months. The Kendal Quaker Charles Gough had died after falling on rocks and his place of death now carries the memorial which was raised at the behest of Canon Rawnsley, then vicar of Crosthwaite church at Keswick and later the founder of the National Trust. Above, in a picture taken on 18 June 1891, Canon Rawnsley can be seen behind the cairn then being built. The photograph is by the famous Ambleside chemist/photographer Herbert Bell, a friend of Canon Rawnsley and a founder of the Armitt Library and Museum at Ambleside, the Wordsworth Museum at Dove Cottage, Grasmere and also of the National Trust. Right, the monumental cairn is seen complete a few years later. Two verses of Wordsworth's eight-verse ode are carved on the slate. (*Above: Bell of Ambleside/J. Marsh Collection. Right: Lowe of Patterdale/J. Marsh Collection*)

Windermere Fire Brigade's decorated horse-drawn fire engine was the winner of the prize for the best decorated vehicle in the Victory Parade following the end of the First World War on 19 August 1919. The fire engine is approaching St Martin's church and is opposite the studio of Herbert and Son, who took pictures of all the procession. Bowness in those days was a more genteel place than today. (*Herbert of Windermere/J. Marsh Collection*)

Bowness-on-Windermere fair on the Glebe attracted many showmen's entertainments. Emerson & Hazard, the famous local fairground people, were the owners of Road Locomotive 'Lightning', which they disposed of in 1913 and replaced with an even more famous engine, Burrell 7hp no. 3562 'Lightning II', which stayed with their fairs until 1948. The author well remembers attending fairs which were lit and powered by the magnificent 'Lightning II', which survives today and can be seen at steam rallies in the north of the country. Here Emerson & Hazard's steam horses entertain the Bowness crowds at a summer fair in 1904. (*Anon/J. Marsh Collection*)

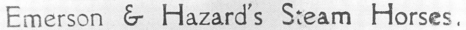

5

*Among the Churches
& Lost Big Houses*

Shap Abbey of God and St Mary Magdalene was Westmorland's only abbey, and thus attracted support from the local famous families. Founded originally on a different site at Preston Patrick in the 1190s by the Premonstratensian (or White) Canons, for a reason not now known, before 1201 the canons had removed their house to a remote valley on the side of the River Lowther near the, even then, ancient settlement of Hepp. The reformation of religion saw the abbey's demise, when along with the other monasteries of Britain it was destroyed to aid the royal coffers in 1540. The site fell into disrepair but part of it became a farm, which is still working today. In the early twentieth century the site was cleaned up by the Ministry of Works and many of the loose stones that can be seen in the photograph were tidied away. Now the site is looked after by the staff of the Lake District National Park as the abbey ruins are just within the National Park: the Lowther, which runs at the east end of the church, is the park boundary. (*Simcoe of Kendal/J. Marsh Collection*)

In this 1930s picture Shap Abbey can be seen in its remote valley, with the River Lowther and the ancient road to the south clearly visible. The 'Magna Strata que venit de Kendal', as the canons of the abbey knew the road, was the medieval equivalent of the M6, as it was the main road from England to Scotland on the west side of the country. Shap Abbey served a useful social purpose as it sheltered travellers over the Shap Fells, which must have been a formidable barrier in medieval times. (*Anon/J. Marsh Collection*)

Shap village had a parish church which was dedicated to St Michael. It was, to quote a guide, 'drastically restored in 1898–99'. The church was a 'spirituality of Shap Abbey' until the reformation and under the authority of Lord Wharton thereafter. The interior of the church before the great Victorian refit is seen here with its three-decker pulpit with oil lamps. The chancel, which was entirely pulled down and rebuilt, can be seen and the wall painting of 'O Be Thankful unto Him' can be seen over the original chancel arch. The box pews are of interest. (*Anon/Wendy Fairer Collection*)

Keld chantry chapel near Shap Abbey is of great interest, not least as a rare survivor of a medieval chantry chapel which became a house, then a barn, and in recent years has been carefully restored by the National Trust. Its proximity to Shap Abbey points to it being part of the religious responsibility of the canons there, but its location as a holy site in almost the centre of Westmorland gives it great importance. Its untidy appearance at the beginning of the twentieth century left a lot to be desired. (*Anon/J. Marsh Collection*)

Morland church, dedicated to St Laurence, has an unknown pre-Norman foundation and is also sited in the centre of the county. Much rebuilt over a thousand years of use, it attracts great interest from architectural historians as a rare and interesting building. In his *Buildings of England* Pevsner says the west tower is the only Anglo-Saxon church tower in Westmorland (or Cumberland), a statement now being contested as early church foundations are being investigated. (*R.K. Dent of Morland/J. Marsh Collection*)

Holy Trinity church, Mardale, being dismantled by the Manchester Corporation Water Engineers in the 1920s/30s is as gloomy a picture as any I possess in my collection. The tiny village church (see opposite) and the hamlet and hotel nearby were all swept away to make a reservoir for the city of Manchester. One of the Manchester Corporation councillors responsible for the destruction took the opportunity of making a few pounds by writing a highly romantic book on Mardale, *A Backwater in Lakeland*. Isaac Hinchliffe JP must go down in Westmorland's history as an author who came and saw and conquered. Plans were well in hand in 1925 when he wrote his half-crown book. He even quoted Keats as an excuse: 'To one who has been long in city spent / 'Tis very sweet to look into the fair / And open face of heaven . . .' These lines open chapter one of a book which is now valued as a last record of a destroyed community. Bits of the church went into a number of other churches in the Carlisle diocese, and stones from the building went into the draw-off tower used at the beginning of the long pipeline to Manchester. Bodies from the churchyard, put there by loving families in their own beautiful family burial ground in their own village, were dug up and put into Shap churchyard. Built in the 1730s, the church hardly saw 200 years of life. (*Anon/J. Marsh Collection*)

Two views of the inside of this tiny church, the dimensions of which are reported to have been 31 × 16 ft (about 10 × 5 metres). The screen, altar rails and gallery date from 1737. The oak pulpit had come from Crosby Ravensworth church. It is of interest to compare these pictures from about 1910 with the picture opposite. 'Let All Thy Works Praise Thee' said the mural at the east end, left to haunt Manchester's workmen. (*Above and below: Anon/J. Marsh Collection*)

Mardale and its church were the subject of many postcard views once the fate being planned for it in Manchester was known. Here we have a Penrith publisher's view of the west end tower – in the 1920s once the centre of village life and soon to be no more. (*Reeds of Penrith/J. Marsh Collection*)

Barton church of St Michael was much rebuilt in 1904, but fortunately the rebuild did not include these ancient arches which support the central tower. Academics say the tower with its arches is early Norman (i.e. late eleventh century) but there is a strong body of opinion that this church was built before the Normans arrived, and that these arches are the remains of a Saxon church. This interior view shows the tower arches and a church lit by oil lamps. The church has gained fame as the 'home' church of William Wordsworth's ancestors, and was much visited by the poet and his sister. (*Anon/J. Marsh Collection*)

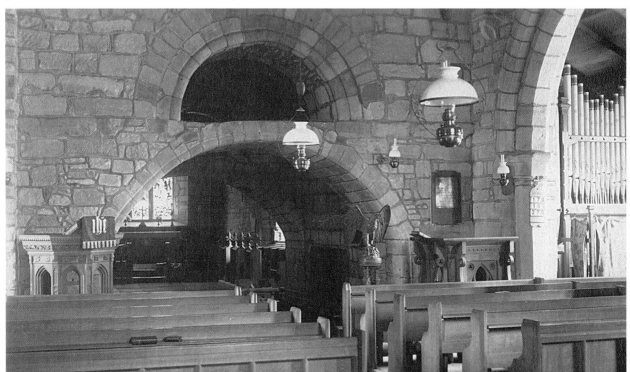

Ambleside and Crook old churches are no more. Above, children play at the gates of St Anne's church at Ambleside, which is reputed to have been built in 1812 on the site of much earlier buildings. This church was replaced in 1854 by a larger one by Sir G. Scott on a site by the river in the valley bottom. The old church was, in due course, converted into residential accommodation. Below, Crook old church was replaced in 1887 by a new building erected nearby against the main road to Windermere. The old church was said to have been built in about 1620 and was possibly on an earlier site. Both churches at Crook share a dedication to St Catherine, a fourth-century saint with a cult dating from the ninth century. There is no doubt that to those interested in early Christian history in Westmorland the ruined tower at Crook, which can still be seen, marks an important archaeological site.
(*Above: Pictorial Stationery Co., London/J. Marsh Collection. Below: Anon/J. Marsh Collection*)

St Mary's church, Crosthwaite, was a chapel of Heversham until 1556, in the middle of the reformation. It was rebuilt in 1626 and 1813 and again in 1877–8. The 1813 version is seen above and was a rather plain building. Below, the 1877 replacement has been photographed from the same roadside location as the top picture, and shows an altogether finer church with an improved tower and an added apse. The nineteenth century saw many old Westmorland churches renewed or replaced; another, at Underbarrow, can be seen opposite. (*Above: Anon/Courtesy of John Gavin. Below: Sawyers of Kendal/J. Marsh Collection*)

All Saints' church, Underbarrow, was rebuilt in 1869 in what Pevsner calls a 'naughty design'. There is no doubt this is an ancient church site but the picture above shows a typical rural church of the seventeenth century. The 1869 church with its 'naughty' features (for example the small tower) is seen photographed from almost the same field position as the earlier view, and confirming that the replacement church was erected on almost exactly the same site as the earlier. (*Above: Anon/Courtesy of the late N. Humphries. Below: Banks of Kendal/J. Marsh Collection*)

St Mark's church, Natland, was a ruin for many years until it was rebuilt in 1735 and 1825. The last of these churches was described as damp and cold, and so a new church was built in 1909 by the locally famous architects Paley & Austin from Lancaster. This church continues in use today as a centre of the growing village. The top picture shows the exterior of the 1825 church, and the lower shows the interior complete with oil lamps. Both pictures are from about 1905. (*Above: Simcoe of Kendal/J. Marsh Collection. Below: Anon/J. Marsh Collection*)

Bowness-on-Windermere church is dedicated to St Martin, one of the most popular of medieval church dedications, one of the earliest being at Whithorn. The Bowness church is also an early Christian foundation, which is attested to by various pieces of stonework that have been found in the building. Above can be seen the exterior of the church in 1869, the year before a large restoration was started; we see below the restored church in about 1905. The electric street lighting is of interest as it indicates the lighting installed, as probably the second installation in the country. The power station was a water-powered generator at Troutbeck Bridge. (*Above: Brunskill of Windermere/J. Marsh Collection. Below: Pictorial Stationery Co., London/J. Marsh Collection*)

The Congregational
chapel in the main
street at Kirkby
Stephen was built in
1864 and became
the Roman Catholic
church of the Holy
Family in 1954. In
September 1986
history was made
here when Prince
Charles, on holiday
in the area with
friends, attended
Mass (the first time
an heir to the
throne had done so
since the sixteenth
century). This
important incident
did nothing for the
history of the
church building, as
it became a shop
when the Catholics
started to share the
parish church for
their services. The
1864 church
continues to this day
in secular use. This
photograph dates
from about 1905.
(*Anon/J. Marsh
Collection*)

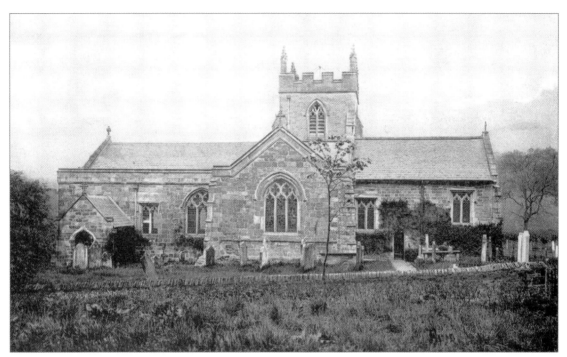

St Michael's in Bongate, Appleby, was as ancient a church as any in the county. There are remains of a Saxon church to be found in the fabric. The church was much restored by the famous Lady of Appleby, Lady Anne Clifford, in about 1659. It is not now a church, having been sold by the diocese in 1978 to be made into a joiner's shop, before it became residential accommodation. The building was mainly fourteenth century and the tower dates from the nineteenth. Above, we see the beautiful proportions of the church in the early 1920s and below, the east end interior is shown as it was at about the same time. The nineteenth-century wall paintings are on both sides of the altar, which dates to the Lady Anne years. A local person remarked to the author, when the church became a workshop, 'Is there nowt sacred any more?', which comment summarises the deteriorating ecclesiastical situation. (*Above: Raphael Tuck/J. Marsh Collection. Below: Valentines of Dundee/J. Marsh Collection*)

Lunefield at Kirkby Lonsdale is now a housing estate but the site was occupied by fine mansions in years gone by. Above we see the original mansion built by Roger Carus in 1815, and pulled down by a new owner in 1869 to be replaced with the Lunefield House seen below, which was built by the architect of the Natural History Museum, Alfred Waterhouse. This larger house for Alfred Harris and family came into the ownership of the Cavendish-Bentinck family from Underley, one branch of which occupied the building until it was given to the Cooperative movement for use as a holiday home. During the Second World War it was occupied by the army, and in 1958, in a tatty state, it was demolished. (*Above: Anon/Kendal Library Collection. Below: Anon/J. Marsh Collection*)

Biggins at Kirkby Lonsdale is also a housing estate, but above we see the last mansion of this name which was built by Dr Paget, who for a time was the medical officer of health for the Westmorland County Council and the founder of the TB sanatorium at Meathop. Built in 1869, it was occupied by the doctor's family until his death in 1937 at the age of eighty-eight. During the war it became the home of an evacuated school from near Blackburn. On 1 January 1943 it was destroyed by fire while most children were away for the Christmas holidays. The top photograph shows the house in its heyday as a school in the early 1940s, and below are the ruins after the fire. The ruined building stood for many years afterwards, but in due course was bought by a developer, who pulled the ruins down and built houses on the site. (*Photographs taken and supplied by Dr V.G. Jolly of Storth*)

Rigmaden, in the Lune valley north of Kirkby Lonsdale, was built in 1825 by Christopher Wilson, and is still owned by the Wilson family, although its history has been bleak in recent years. Above we see the large mansion as it was until the Second World War, when the family were having difficulty with the fabric. Pevsner described it in 1967 as 'in ruins' but in the early 1990s there was a restoration, which is pictured below. The lower picture shows how the centre of the original house had been cleared away, leaving the two ends to be developed as housing units. The author attended an open day when the Wilson family described their plans for the renewal of this Webster of Kendal building. (*Above: Anon/J. Marsh Collection. Below: J. Marsh/J. Marsh Collection*)

Grimeshill at Middleton in the Lune valley was the home of the lords of the manor for many years but, in common with the owners of many other big houses, the family suffered in the depression of the 1920s and 1930s. As was the case with the nearby mansion at Rigmaden, rot set into the fabric to such an extent that the building had to be pulled down. In 1936 Robert Blades, the last gardener at the estate, took the top picture before he joined the armed forces. In 1939, as the war was about to start, he returned on leave and took the picture below of the house being demolished. The house front is shown in both pictures. The Moore family had lived at Grimeshill since 1701, but the male line expired in 1909 when William Middleton-Moore died, leaving a widow who lived on in the house into the 1930s. The top picture was taken just before she died. Another sad Westmorland story. (*Above and below: The late Robert Blades/J. Marsh Collection*)

Brougham Hall is in the north of the county on the outskirts of Penrith, then in Cumberland. It was the home of the Lords Brougham who mainly built the fine mansion that is shown here. The top picture shows Brougham Hall in about 1905, from the extensive lawns which are now part of a housing estate, and below is the west terrace with the bridge to the Brougham chapel. When the last Lord Brougham to inherit the hall lost his fortune through gambling, the occupier of Carleton Hall took the opportunity to buy Brougham Hall, then known as the Windsor of the north, and pull it down as he had no time for the Broughams. Westmorland County Council managed to stop this destruction, but most of the house was down by the time of their intervention. Little remains today, although there are plans by a small group of people to restore the hall to its former glory. Their efforts are proceeding slowly: the hall today is surrounded by a high-class housing estate and a number of businesses have found homes in the ruined fabric. Not exactly what could be called a restoration. (*Above: Anon/J. Marsh Collection. Below: Reed of Penrith/J. Marsh Collection*)

Dalton Hall was the seat of the lord of the manor for Burton in Kendal, and when the author went to live in Burton in 1961 the hall and its estate were still functioning as they had ever done. The staff had been reduced from its size in Victorian days but the Mason-Hornby family were still held in high regard by the tenants and villagers. Over the next five years the decline of the hall became very obvious. It was let to tenants, but developed serious dry rot – which meant it had to be taken down. The Mason-Hornbys lived in a caravan nearby while a new house of much neater proportions was built on the site; the family lives there today. The first Dalton Hall was in a nearby house, which became a farmhouse and is now known as Dalton Old Hall. It was replaced in the eighteenth century by a new Dalton Hall, which was rebuilt in 1859 as the hall seen in these two pictures: a view of the hall from the nearby hill in the park, and the west front, with access to all of the main rooms through a garden door. (*Above and below: Rowbothams of Burton/J. Marsh Collection*)

Arnside had a big house called Inglemere, which was built in 1882 to be 'the occasional residence of Mr R.F. Thompson, Solicitor of Kendal'. In fact it was too large. When Mrs Innes acquired the house she extended it to make a boarding school for girls, but when she remarried in the 1930s to become Mrs Llewellyn the house was changed into a hotel, and so it remained until it was demolished in recent years to make room for a housing estate. The top picture is of the house as a hotel with a putting green, and the lower picture is of the back of the house as a school, with tennis courts. Inglemere did not have a long history as anything, house, school or hotel, but the name remains on the housing estate that replaced it. The gateposts to the drive can be seen today as an entrance to the estate on Arnside Hill. (*Above: R.A. Series, London/J. Marsh Collection. Below: Turners of Skipton/J. Marsh Collection*)

6

Kendal – Not the County Town

Kendal's moot hall in Stricklandgate was an amazing survivor from the days of the Elizabethan foundation of a Royal Borough, as it was built in the sixteenth century to house the new council of burgesses, and also the law courts for the area. It was still possible, just before this photograph was taken, to see the large courtroom where much of the history of sixteenth- to nineteenth-century Kendal was recorded. The ground floor had become a shop after the disposal of the building when the Borough Council and the courts moved to the new Town Hall on the Highgate/Lowther Street corner. When the shop was burgled in the 1960s the criminal allegedly set fire to the building to hide his fingerprints. Kendal lost one of its most historic buildings. The concrete and breeze block replacement has little to commend it beyond a slight similarity to the original. Here the building is fully ablaze and an unfortunate accident had just occurred: a fireman had fallen off the ladder. (*Anon/J. Marsh Collection*)

Many of Kendal's ancient and interesting buildings have been swept away in the cause of commercial enterprise over many years, even before the arrival of 'the planners'. Above, the Castle Dairy is the oldest of Kendal's secular buildings, dating back to the thirteenth or fourteenth century and continuously occupied ever since. There was an attempt to pull it down to expand a tractor business in the 1930s but an outcry led by the local antiquarian society caused that plan to be dropped. The picture dates from about 100 years ago. Below is the house in which George Romney died in 1802. It has been refaced since that date but that is probably the only assault on it since it was built. Both these buildings are amazing survivors. (*Above and below: Judges of Hastings/J. Marsh Collection*)

Kendal Holy Trinity church, built in the thirteenth century (it is guessed), did not escape the desire of the Victorians to change everything. In the early 1850s it was almost completely demolished and rebuilt so what we see today, externally, dates from that period. Above is the rebuilt church in about 1900 on the river side. Next to it is the old vicarage (eighteenth century and earlier), which was demolished to make way for a parish hall. Below, the interior of the church has been much changed since this picture was taken in about 1900, and much of the woodwork put in to replace medieval screens has also been replaced, as the altar has been moved about to satisfy fashion in various periods. The stories told by the workmen who installed the central heating and lowered the medieval floor, regarding discoveries made, point to complete irresponsibility by the church authorities of the time – and more loss to Kendal and Westmorland. (*Above and below: Stengal, London/J. Marsh Collection*)

Two features on the River Kent in Kendal that are no more are featured here. Above can be seen the Netherbridge ford, which dates back to the earliest days of Kendal. When Nether Bridge was built in medieval times it was known as the Caput Pontis (the head bridge), but it was built as a narrow river crossing that required the continued use of the ford adjacent to it for wide vehicles, which were few, and herds and flocks of animals, which were many. The final vestiges of the ford were swept away when the river was widened and deepened during flood prevention work in the 1970s. The old cottages and the lodge that was built at the entrance to the old vicarage's drive had been pulled down some time before the flood prevention work. Below can be seen the Lound 'dam', which was in fact a weir on the river to divert water on to the leet to the Low Mills on the Natland Road. As the Low Mills no longer needed water power and the weir actually held water back, the last remaining bits of the Lound dam were removed when the river was widened to prevent flooding. (*Above and below: Anon/J. Marsh Collection*)

The Kendal Horse Fair is now no longer held, unlike Appleby annual horse fair which attracts much attention from the romantics. A feature of the fairs was the entertainment which was provided for visitors. In Kendal this continues today on the same site on the riverside at New Road. These two photographs from about 1900 show the entertainment coinciding with flooding. In the top picture Matilda Hoardley's 'three abreast gallopers' and Murphy's gondolas can be seen in full swing as the river rises, and below, the river has engulfed the site, and the fair equipment is being cleared. (*Above and below: Anon/G. Dawson Collection*)

The Kendal time gun was a feature of South Westmorland life from the early nineteenth century. It was fired at one o'clock every day, which was a boon for the many who did not have clocks. The first cannon used was mounted on a plinth in the Serpentine Woods, which was owned by the Kendal Fell Trust. It was fired by hand and the sound could be heard for many miles around. In due course this large cannon was taken down to the Abbot Hall Park where, mounted on a suitable carriage, it was a feature for many years. The replacement gun was something about the size of a starting gun for boat races, and this was fired electrically from a jeweller and clock merchants at the top of Finkle Street. This gun was stolen in the 1960s and the interesting custom came to an end. Above we see the first gun in the Serpentine woods in about 1900, and below, a decade or so later, it is in Abbot Hall Park. The original gun was taken away as wartime scrap, along with the railings that can also be seen. (*Above: Stengal of London/J. Marsh Collection. Below: Anon/J. Marsh Collection*)

The Highgate yards in Kendal were swept away in a postwar frenzy of destruction planned to tidy up the town. Planners fresh from university courses in 'town planning' were let loose on the Auld Grey Town and much was lost, as Dr Starkey recently commented. Above can be seen Braithwaite's woollen mill, which escaped the planners by being burnt down in suspicious circumstances. The small cottage adjoining is now all that is left of the buildings in this picture. Below, the last of the Kendal handloom weavers had his premises in a Highgate yard that is no more. Here Mr Dixon is pictured at his loom, which can now be seen in the Museum of Lakeland Life at Abbot Hall in Kendal. (*Above and right: Anon/ J. Marsh Collection*)

Acknowledgements

The production of this book would not have been possible without the assistance of the following people, many of whom have let me use their family photographs to bring together a unique collection of material. In recent years so many of them have died that the inclusion of their material contributes to a memorial to their lives in Westmorland. The late Mr Robert Blades, Dr V.G. Jolly, the late Olive Wilson, the late John Story, George Dawson, who deserves special mention for his continued generosity over many years, Mrs Leonora Knowles, Preston Whiteley, who always allows use of his railway photographs which are unique records of a long gone railway system, Neville Stead of Whitley Bay, Mrs Hodgson of Langdale, the late Mrs Taylor of Crosthwaite, the late William Hoggarth of Burton in Kendal, the late Abigail Reed of Kendal, the late Mrs Baker of Kendal, Mrs G. Carrick, Holme Local History Society, Mr D.M. Williams, one-time Kirkby Stephen chemist, Mr Dobson of Troutbeck Bridge, Ms Wendy Fairer of Shap, John Gavin of Ambleside who gave so much of his life to the Armitt Trust, the late N. Humphries and the Local Studies collection of the Kendal Library and Mrs Jackie Fay, librarian in charge.